Beautiful Things Happen

WHEN A WOMAN TRUSTS GOD

SHEILA WALSH

THOMAS NELSON
Since 1798

NASHVILLE   DALLAS   MEXICO CITY   RIO DE JANEIRO

This book is dedicated in loving memory of Jim Martin of Ayr, Scotland who showed me an unwavering picture of what it looks like to trust God every day of your life.

Published in Nashville, Tennessee, by Thomas Nelson. Thomas Nelson is a registered trademark of Thomas Nelson, Inc.

Thomas Nelson, Inc., titles may be purchased in bulk for educational, business, fund-raising, or sales promotional use. For information, please e-mail SpecialMarkets@ThomasNelson.com.

All Scripture quotations, unless otherwise indicated, are taken from THE NEW KING JAMES VERSION. © 1982 Thomas Nelson Publishers. Used by permission. All rights reserved.

Other Scripture quotations are taken from the following sources:

The Message (MSG) by Eugene H. Peterson. © 1993, 1994, 1995, 1996, 2000, 2001, 2002. Used by permission of NavPress Publishing Group. All rights reserved. The *Holy Bible*, New Living Translation (NLT). © 1996, 2004. Used by permission of Tyndale House Publishers, Inc., Wheaton, Illinois 60189. All rights reserved. THE ENGLISH STANDARD VERSION (ESV). © 2001 by Crossway Bibles, a division of Good News Publishers. THE GOOD NEWS TRANSLATION (GNT). © 1976, 1992 by The American Bible Society. Used by permission. All rights reserved. THE HOLY BIBLE: NEW INTERNATIONAL VERSION® (NIV). © 1973, 1978, 1984 by International Bible Society. Used by permission of Zondervan Publishing House. All rights reserved. THE NEW AMERICAN STANDARD BIBLE® (NASB), © The Lockman Foundation 1960, 1962, 1963, 1968, 1971, 1972, 1973, 1975, 1977, 1995. Used by permission.

ISBN 978-1-4002-8090-2 (IE)

Library of Congress Cataloging-in-Publication Data

Walsh, Sheila, 1956–
  Beautiful things happen when a woman trusts God / Sheila Walsh.
    p. cm.
  ISBN 978-1-4002-0243-0
  1. Christian women—Religious life. 2. Trust in God. I. Title.
  BV4527.W347 2009
  248.8'43—dc22

2009047812

Printed in the United States of America

10 11 12 13 14 WC 9 8 7 6 5 4 3

Contents

Acknowledgments

I would like to thank the following people who worked side by side with me on this project.

Kathie Johnson, thank you for all the editorial support that made this book possible.

Jennifer Stair, thank you for your careful attention to detail and flow. You have the gift of being able to polish the words while retaining the heart of the message.

Jeanette Thomason, when Jennifer and I were finished you took our work, sat with it for a while, and when you returned it, I was tempted to shout "touchdown!" You cleared the path of any superfluous rubble so that all that mattered was all that remained.

Bryan Norman, it is pure joy to work with you! Apart from being an exceptionally gifted and insightful editor you are such a fun friend.

Michael Hyatt and the team at Thomas Nelson, it is a privilege to be a part of your family of creative thinkers and writers.

Mary Graham and Women of Faith, for the past fourteen years we have been on a journey together connecting women to a God who loves them passionately and to one another. I love you all.

Author's Note

Fifteen years ago, life as I knew it came to an end. Everything I had built came crashing to the ground, crushing me beneath the rubble. A few friends tried to pull me from the ruins, but I had no desire to be saved. I wanted to be left alone to die.

Into that darkest of nights came the Son of God. In that moment, he didn't come to me as Savior or Liberator or King—he came as the Lamb who stayed beside me through long, dark days and nights. His presence was deeply comforting. He let me bury my face in his wool and weep. He let me lay my head by his and sleep.

One day, he stood up and I stood beside him. He began to make his way out of the ruins, into the daylight. I didn't want to leave and begged him to stay, but he kept walking. I followed. I never wanted to be separated from him.

As we stood in the sunlight, I found the vista before me terrifying. "I can't do this," I said.

I know, he answered.

"I don't want to do this," I said.

I know, he answered.

"What will I do?" I asked.

Just follow me, he said.

"Where are we going?" I asked.

We're going home.

INTRODUCTION

Swinging in the Arms of God

July 7, 1966, The Swing. When I was a child, my mom would take my sister Frances and me to the swings in the park. I loved being pushed on the swing by someone I trusted. I felt as if I were flying, airborne, without a care in the world. I would cry out, "Higher, Mommy, higher!"

I remember one day, though, when it was just my big sister and me at the park. Frances pushed me on my swing for a while and then got tired and sat down on the grass. A boy who was known as the neighborhood bully came up behind me and began to push my swing. I was terrified. He wasn't pushing it any higher than my sister had, but I didn't trust him. I cried and cried until my sister told him to stop.

The matter, you see, came down to a five-letter word: trust. Trust made flying high in the air an exhilarating experience, and when trust was absent, the swing turned into a nightmare. Who was pushing the swing made all the difference in the world. The heart behind the hands pushing the swing changed everything.

September 19, 1992, The Hospital. I sat in my car in the parking lot outside a drugstore in Washington, D.C. In my hand was a prescription for a medication treating clinical depression, and I wasn't sure what I was going to do with it. Every morning in the hospital, I had lined up with the other patients to receive my meds in a little plastic cup. Now I was on my own and it was up to me whether I took the antidepressant or not.

When I was discharged that morning, I had to answer a few standard questions.

"Do you have suicidal thoughts?"

"No."

"Do you have an appointment with a doctor in your area when you return to Virginia Beach?"

"Yes, I do."

"Are you familiar with the signs of an oncoming downward spiral?"

"Yes, I am."

I signed a few papers and a girl at the discharge desk returned my car keys to me. That was it. The simplicity of that gesture seemed out of place with the enormity of what I felt. For the first two weeks of my monthlong stay, I had to sign a paper to get my hair dryer out of a locked cupboard; now I was being trusted with a car. The hospital was done with me, and new patients were being admitted. I felt a little put out by the whole affair. I thought of yelling, "I'm still nuts, you know. I see dead dogs walking!" but reconsidered.

A cold wind had caught me by surprise as I walked out of the hospital into the parking lot. It was October and very chilly. Just a month before, I had been terrified to walk through those doors. Now I felt very vulnerable having left the safety and companionship I had found there.

I decided to spend the night in a hotel before driving the three hours to Virginia Beach the following day. My only task for the evening was to fill my prescription at a local drugstore. As I sat there I thought, *What if someone recognizes me and asks what I'm doing? What if they ask an innocent question like, "Did you get strep throat, too?" What will I say?*

The truth was I was still ashamed that I needed pills to live a "normal" life. I had resisted the psychiatrist's therapeutic diagnosis in the hospital at first.

"I don't want some 'happy' pill," I said.

He was gentle with my ignorance and took time to explain that rather than this being a "happy" pill, it was medication to help my brain function normally. "Your brain is not producing enough serotonin, a necessary chemical for proper brain function, which is why you are having trouble thinking clearly and sleeping at night."

Reluctantly, I began to take the medication, and within a few days I could tell a significant difference. The most obvious was that I stopped crying all the time! I began to feel the faintest touch of hope again. Perhaps somehow God would walk me through this labyrinth of despair after all.

It's one thing, though, to line up with others who are waiting for their meds; it's quite another when you are abruptly thrust back into the regular population. I was acutely aware of the stigma attached to any kind of mental illness, and I didn't have the words, the strength, or the heart to explain to someone else why I needed this little blue pill.

"I don't like this, Lord. This is not what I thought my life would look like," I prayed in my car.

In my heart, I heard him answer: *I know, Sheila. Just follow me.*

August 4, 2008, The Waiting Room. The waiting room seemed carefully designed to send a message to young or old: *You are okay; this is normal.* In one corner were children's books and toys, a table and four chairs designed for little legs. In the other corner: a sofa and a coffee table with magazines—from *Sports Illustrated* to women's magazines showing the latest fashions draped on ridiculously skinny girls. But the fact remained: this was a psychiatrist's office, and no potted plant or magazine could dress up that reality.

I pressed a button on the wall next to the doctor's name, and a little red light flashed. I assumed the same indicator went on inside his office to let him know that his next patient had arrived. As I waited, all I could think was, *What am I doing here?* I'd done my time. I'd taken my pills. Why was I back in one more soothingly decorated room preparing for yet another psychiatrist's appointment?

A door opened and a man I took to be in his early forties looked at me. "Sheila?" he asked.

I followed him through the door, past other closed doors, and into his office. He asked if I'd like something to drink, but I told him I was fine.

"So what brought you here today?" he asked kindly.

I almost laughed. I wanted to say, "How long have you got?" but I knew the answer. Fifty minutes would be the most he could spare. Instead I cut to the chase. "It's kind of a long story," I said. "Just think of me as a kid who used to love being pushed on a swing until she discovered that swings are not safe."

"Swings?" he inquired.

"Well, that's just a starting point, I guess. What I mean is that I went on to discover that life is not safe."

Do You Trust Me?

I see these moments now as little movies in my head. I can still picture my childhood park and old, rusty swings, and I can remember the fear I felt that day. That fear was a prelude to some of the bigger moments in life when it felt as if fear might literally consume me.

The truth is that these moments and feelings have always been about the same thing, and I can reduce them to one question, not from a doctor but from God, my Father: *Sheila, do you trust me?*

I have answered yes many times, only to discover that the question is so much bigger than I ever imagined.

So this is a book about trust: how hard it is to trust, how we learn to trust, how we live with trust, and how our lives are transformed by trust. It is a book about how trust turns nightmares into exhilarating moments when we are fully convinced of the trustworthiness of the one who is moving our lives along. It is about how trust is the greatest gift that we can give our Father—a gift of immeasurable beauty.

The Rest of My Story

Fifteen years ago I wrote the book *Honestly*[1] to tell the story of my journey from television talk-show host and singer to the locked ward of a psychiatric hospital where I struggled with a crippling depression. To someone who had lived her life desperately trying to do the right thing, to be the right thing, it was terrifying to find myself in a psychiatric hospital. At the worst moment of my life when everything that made sense to me was gone, Jesus called me to stand beside him.

Learning to start again is not easy. I had to relearn how to be a daughter and sister, a wife and mother, and a friend. Just as a child learns to walk by falling down and getting back up again, I had to learn that every fall was a gift and every bruise a sign that I was alive and moving. *Honestly* told the beginnings of this journey.

Now, fifteen years later, I'd like to tell the rest of my story.

What has surprised me along the way is that I thought that this was my story alone.

It's not. I am only one among thousands of others whom Jesus has called and continues to call back from fear to faith, from being crippled by doubt to being liberated by trust.

I have a feeling that as you hold this book, you are not sure you want to know how this journey looks. You may fear the pain will overwhelm you. To that fear, with which I am so familiar, I can say that learning to trust changes everything; no matter how painful the transformation, you will not regret a moment lived, tear shed, or fear faced along the way.

That's because when you are called out of crippling fear, you are not returned to business as usual. You will be amazed at what God has planned for you. There is a world of breathtaking wonder wrapped up in trusting God with everything you have and everything you are. You will discover that you are free!

Never in a million years could I have anticipated what this journey would look like for me. Take a look.

That fall 1992, Jesus called me to walk a path out of the wreckage of my former life, going from talk-show host to patient in a psychiatric ward. That was decidedly a shock, but only the beginning. I've since learned that Jesus wants me to trust him so completely that I no longer question anything he puts into my hands or the path he chooses for my life.

Ten people have shown me that in significant, powerful ways, and you will meet them throughout this book. Each time I came to a roadblock or unfamiliar territory in my life, one of these men or women waited to teach me what I needed to learn before I could move on. You may recognize some of these people's names, but their stories are sure to surprise you. They have taught me that not only is it safe to swing in the arms of God, but beautiful things happen when we trust him.

Through the prophetess Anna, I learned that sometimes we have to wait a lifetime to see the fulfillment of a dream, and part of the gift is who we became in the process of waiting. When we wait and trust in God's presence, we become more like Christ and that is beautiful.

For a while I sat with Mary and Martha. I'd seen their tears flow at the death of their brother, Lazarus, but what arrested me was seeing their confusion and hurt at how long it took Jesus to get to them. I recognized those feelings. Have you been there, needing God to do something but it's as if he's not listening to you? Mary and Martha learned how trust can call us into dark places where it seems as if God is doing nothing—and that is never true. Their story, perhaps more than any, has given me courage to stand fast when all looks lost. God is always there and we are never lost.

Then there's the apostle Paul, a man convinced he was right when he was dead wrong. Paul threw himself passionately into eradicating a new sect of God's chosen called "the Way," only to discover that he was persecuting the Lamb of God. Paul was plunged into physical blindness for days, but I imagine the internal darkness was far worse. In the end, he became a man of grace, and his message to us is that there is nothing good in any of us apart from Christ. If you have ever made a very bad decision that seems to be your utter ruin, lean in and look at Paul. When you come out of this dark place, you will be a different woman, loving God with a passion you never knew was possible.

Perhaps you are the quiet one in your crowd of friends, the one who doesn't wait to be asked to help. You anticipate and get the job done, you trust God to use it all for his purposes, but sometimes you wonder if your life makes much of a difference at all. Tabitha was such a woman who quietly served all her life—and then, one day, was gone. Her death was a shock to her friends, who one by one told Peter what she had done for them, how she had woven love and service into their lives. While I'm not sure Tabitha thought of herself as beautiful, those around her did.

I think I am more like Gideon than Tabitha. At certain moments in my life I've felt God calling me to places I didn't want to go because others would do a better job than I would. At this point in my life, I'm finally getting it: there will always be those who can do things better but God chooses each of us to show what he can do. I titled this book *Beautiful Things Happen When a Woman Trusts God* because I see that in my life—the way God took a scared little girl and kept calling me to follow him and see where he was going.

Then we will meet Joseph. I thought I knew his story but there is so much I have missed. For me, the greatest gift from Joseph's story is seeing that as we learn to trust God, we can let others off the hook. The more we believe that God is in control, the more we can forgive others for the pain they have caused us. This is huge! Carrying bitterness in our hearts eradicates the beauty of Christ, but letting it go brings peace—and we can let go because no matter what others intended for evil, God will work for good. This one lesson can change our lives forever. Can you see the beauty that God works in us when we trust him?

But what if you are a woman who has failed God over and over, and all you can think right now is that these accounts are too little and too late? You will be encouraged by Samson's story. Samson was a man who had it all. He was chosen by God, raised by trusting parents, and called to be a leader—and he blew it all because of passion for a woman. That was his greatest downfall, but he also made lots of poor choices all along the way. At the end of his life, as he was faced with the public humiliation of where his choices had taken him, he reached out to God one more time and God caught him. He shows us how it is never too late to trust one more time. Even if you have only one breath left in your body, God can make it beautiful.

Perhaps it's hard for you to openly trust God because of the place you hold in your community or office. You would like to be a light in a dark place, but it might cost too much. Nicodemus wrestled with that. He wanted to make sure that Jesus was who he claimed to be, so he went to talk to him—at night, when the conversation could be inconspicuous. Ultimately, he found out what martyred missionary Jim Elliot discovered and as his wife Elisabeth shared in *The Shadow of the Almighty*, "He is no fool who gives what he cannot keep to gain that which he cannot lose."

One of the most compelling lives we will look at is that of Abraham. He is the only one in the Bible called God's friend. What a beautiful description. I find his story very encouraging as it shows us the progression of trust. Abraham didn't start out a trusting man—he took little steps of trust initially, would fall, and then get back up again to take the next step. His life became a thing of beauty along the way.

So, those are our traveling companions. I trust that you will find yourself in the pages of this book, but more than that I trust and pray that you will see that as you learn to trust God more and more, beautiful things will happen in and through your life.

ONE

Why Are You So Afraid?

The Beauty of Courage

Relying on God has to begin all over again
every day as if nothing had yet been done.

—C. S. Lewis

This is the way God works. Over and over again He
pulls our souls back from certain destruction so
we'll see the light—and live in the light!

—Job 33:29–30 MSG

Back home in Virginia Beach after being released from the psychiatric hospital, I began to see a therapist, initially three times a week: Dr. Frank Gripka. This kind, gracious, gray-haired gentleman had a profound impact on my life, an impact that continues to this day. One of the most powerful things he said to me was, "Sheila, Jesus didn't come to get you out of the pain of life; he has come to live *in you* through it."

That one statement alone was worth months of therapy.

I began to realize that my prayers had been focused on getting through this difficult time and returning to whatever kind of normal I could find. I wanted this disruption to be over. I wanted to feel better, to be happy again. I had prayed that Jesus would "fix me" so that no one else would know what was true about my story. I didn't want to be the girl with the kind of issues that made people whisper.

Only that "normal," shiny, controlled, pre-disrupted life would be shallow, Dr. Gripka was showing me.

Slowly I began to embrace the truth that my life was no longer mine to control. I belonged to Christ, and he wanted to live his life through me—through the good days and the difficult ones too. This fresh understanding gave me the courage to do the thing I feared most: to listen to what other key people in my life had to say to me. I didn't want that. I didn't want people seeing all my doubts, fears, and uncontrollable imperfections. I wanted to run away and start a new life somewhere else where no one knew me, where I could be just the girl with the funny accent, a cat, and no past.

How Long Are You Going to Run?

That was when one of my closest friends, Steve Lorenz, challenged me. I still remember that day. I was very upset by a phone call I had received. The caller, someone I knew, said that they heard from a reliable source that I had quit my job and was running away from anyone having any input into my life. I was hurt because this person didn't ask me what was going on and simply believed what someone else supposed. I wanted the caller's and my history together to mean something—enough to give me the benefit of the doubt. Never mind that there was some truth to what the caller had said. I just shut down. I felt physically too weak to deal with any criticism. I called Steve, in a panic, hardly able to breathe.

"Sheila," he asked, "how long are you going to run? When will you stand still and see that God is with you? Why are you so afraid of what other people think?"

Why indeed? It was true that I had built my security on what other people thought. I couldn't deny to Steve what my actions told both of us, that I believed if the person on the phone thought I was flaky, that had to be true.

Steve reinforced what Dr. Gripka had said: I was being called to stand still, confident that Jesus was with me. I had nothing to be afraid of, especially the truth. Steve also reminded me that walking away from what I am afraid of doesn't make it go away. I had to feel and face the fear. I had to know I was not alone.

I read the truth of this that night in the book of Isaiah—another of the awesome promises about the coming King: "A bruised reed he will not break, and a smoldering wick he will not snuff out" (42:3 NIV).

Either Way I'm in Trouble

Certainly I was feeling very bruised and close to broken. It seemed to me that there were those around me who would gladly snuff me out. In fact, in the days leading up to my time in the hospital, I had tried to find out how a diagnosis of clinical depression would be viewed, and discovered that mental illness is very controversial in many areas of the church. Not everyone acknowledges the validity of clinical depression as an illness, seeing it instead as a lack of faith, a surrender to weakness, or an indication of some secret sin. I had worked with some people during those five years whom I considered friends only to discover that when I needed them most, they were not only distant but also dismissive. One staff member went as far as to tell my boss, Dr. Pat Robertson, that he considered me to be a pathological liar who was making up everything for sympathy and attention.

I cannot describe how betrayed and wounded I felt. I was already low, not sleeping or eating well, and overwhelmingly sad. I found myself wondering if they were right. *What if I was imagining this illness to excuse myself from being a responsible adult?* That agony was the final straw that caused me to seek help.

I sat in Dr. Robertson's office one day and said, "I don't know what's true anymore. If those who are standing against me are right, then I need help. If what I am experiencing is legitimate, then I also need help. Either way, I'm in trouble."

When I returned to Virginia Beach after the monthlong hospitalization, Dr. Robertson was kind enough to offer to find me a job at CBN until I felt well enough to be back on-air, but I knew that wasn't the best option for me then. I had a lot of things I needed to work through. I wanted to understand why I was so afraid of what other people thought of me. I needed to resolve the anger and hurt I felt toward those whom I felt betrayed me.

I also wanted to find out why, for as long as I can remember, I have been waiting for the other shoe to drop.

Perhaps you know that feeling. It's an insidious intruder that whispers to us whenever we begin to feel hope again. For me, I was afraid to be happy, because I assumed at that very moment I finally found happiness, there would be a thud.

Facing My Fear

I spent a lot of time meeting with those who felt I had let them down and those I felt had dismissed me. The fresh realization that God knew my story and loved me gave me the ability to open up to the input of others. My heart at every meeting was to listen so I didn't defend myself. I simply listened to what the person in front of me was saying and tried to put myself in their shoes.

I was fascinated by the power of listening; it became a very revealing exercise that I continue to this day. I discovered that when I am defensive, I am deaf; but when I have an open heart, I can hear clearly.

Still, not every meeting ended as I hoped. There were many tears shed. At the end of some meetings, I was sad but not destroyed. It may seem strange to you to think that a grown woman would feel so helpless against the opinions of others. The truth is, there was a wounded child inside me who at times still liked to take center stage. I was learning to bring that part of me to the feet of Jesus to be healed and loved out of shame.

Though I did give opportunities to everyone who felt they needed to say something to me, I did not let every Tom, Dick, or Harriet dump his or her personal preferences or beliefs on me. The people I sat with were those I had a real relationship with; integrity called for accountability. It was a very cleansing pursuit. It felt good to be responsible for my choices and take ownership of my own life. After several weeks of counseling and conversations, I knew that it was time to take a next step. I knew that I didn't want to return to the spotlight, so I began to ask God what that next step should be.

For too long I have tried to dance one beat ahead of time, yet deep inside an ancient song sings to this soul of mine and told me not to be afraid of things that shadow me. In facing them at last, I will be free.

January 26, 1993

New Beginnings

As I asked God for direction, I was drawn toward attending seminary. I applied to the master's program at Fuller Seminary in Southern California and was accepted. Just a few weeks later, in the spring of 1993, I packed up everything I wanted to take with me in my white car and set off on a 2,736 mile journey from Virginia Beach to Southern California.

I love to drive and enjoyed every moment of the trip. I didn't rush. I spent a night with my friends Bill and Gloria Gaither in Indiana, and took time to drive over the breathtaking Rocky Mountains in Colorado. I even spent one night in Las Vegas. (One night seemed to suffice for one who had been raised as a Baptist.)

I will never forget the first moment that I caught a glimpse of the Pacific Ocean. Tears rolled down my cheeks, and I knew that for the moment at least, I was home. I grew up by the ocean, and it has always felt like home to me. I find something so comforting about the ocean. Whether it's the beautiful sun-kissed Pacific or the wild green and gray of the Atlantic, the beauty and vastness of the oceans move me deeply.

I loved California: the weather, the scenery, and the water. I lived as close to the beach as I could afford, which means if you stood on the balcony of my small apartment with strong binoculars on a clear day, you could just about see the sun paint a ribbon of color across the ocean. I loved my apartment in Laguna Niguel. It was full of everything that had meaning for me: good books, music, family photos, black-and-white posters of London and Paris.

I also had a cat named Abigail. Every time I watched Abigail wash her paws and clean her fur, I saw a picture of myself. Having come through such a dark time, my small sanctuary in Laguna Niguel seemed to be a place to lick my wounds and recover. I quickly settled into my apartment and life as a seminary student, and weeks turned to months.

All seemed quiet on my new western front. I would have been quite happy for it to stay that way, but there was a change in the air. I didn't feel it until it was right upon me.

An Open Door

The Beauty of Brokenness

I suppose when we wake on January 1 the world will look the same. But there is a reminder of the Resurrection at the start of each New Year, each new decade. That's why I also like sunrises, Mondays, and new seasons. God seems to be saying, "With me you can always start afresh."

—Ada Lum

Do not remember the former things, nor consider the things of old. Behold, I will do a new thing, now it shall spring forth; shall you not know it?

—Isaiah 43:18–19

One sunny morning, I was sitting out on my balcony with a cup of coffee in front of me, Abigail on my lap, and my Bible open to the book of the prophet Isaiah. I found such comfort in a particular passage that I underlined the verses:

> Fear not, for I have redeemed you; I have called you by your name; you are Mine. When you pass through the waters, I will be with you; and through the rivers, they shall not overflow you. When you walk through the fire, you shall not be burned, nor shall the flame scorch you. For I am the LORD your God, The Holy One of Israel, your Savior. (43:1–3)

As I read on, I came to a couple of verses I just couldn't get past. I read them over and over, each time arrested by something in the text that felt deeper than my immediate understanding:

> Do not remember the former things, nor consider the things of old. Behold, I will do a new thing, now it shall spring forth; shall you not know it? (43:18–19)

At first, I looked at the obvious new things in my life. I was living in a new place. I was a new student in seminary. I had just met and was dating a great guy, Barry. But none of these realities felt as if they fit the weight of what God was speaking to me. So I underlined the verses, marked the date—March 5, 1993—and let it rest.

The following year was full of discovery. I was surprised and happy that I could still learn new things. Since one of the side effects of clinical depression can be short-term memory loss, I worried that I wouldn't be able to retain what I was learning in my first class at Fuller Seminary.

Then I discovered a great friend in Barry. As our friendship began to grow into something deeper, I found myself wondering if I was too fragile to form a serious relationship. I had never allowed myself before to feel fragile—I wanted to see myself as a strong person, someone others could lean upon. Now I was learning things about myself that belied that myth. I was finding out that my only true strength was in following Jesus, trusting him, and leaning on him. So after a series of on-again, off-again moments in my relationship with Barry, it became clear to me that he was a good man and my love for him began to grow. What really mattered to me was that he and I were on the same path and we were following the same Shepherd. We both knew brokenness and healing. That seemed to be the hallmark of every new relationship I was making.

Part of learning to trust God was learning to trust that he would lead me and keep me on not necessarily an easy path but a safe one. I had spent the previous thirty-six years charging ahead, confident that I knew what I was doing. Now I was very much in the shoes of a child, learning to take one step at a time; as a child looks into the eyes of her mother to see if she's doing it right, I set my gaze on my heavenly Father. I knew that he would catch me if I fell.

It was clear to me that many of the friendships and relationships I had formed in the past were based on what I believed I could offer someone. Now my heart was tuned to find others who were following after the Shepherd in simple trust.

One of my fondest moments of that time is the gift of my friendship with Frank and Marlene Rice. Marlene got my telephone number from a mutual friend and called me to suggest we meet for lunch. From that first meeting I knew we'd be friends for life. Marlene is funny and kind and a little eccentric. She has a passion to share the love of Christ at every opportunity. At that time, Marlene worked with Open Doors with Brother Andrew, an organization supporting the persecuted church around the world.

I liked the fact that she was deeply spiritual but not in the least judgmental. I had no way of knowing that God was about to use her to open a door to a new resurrected life.

Bottom of the Barrel

The phone rang one morning as I was rushing out the door to get to class. I almost let the machine take it, but as all my family live in Scotland and England, I never want to miss a chance to hear their voices. It was Marlene.

"Sheila, I need you to do me a favor," she said.

"Sure. Just name it; what do you need?"

"I need you to speak at a women's luncheon at a country club in Palm Springs on Saturday."

I laughed. "I would rather stick my hand in a blender than do that!"

Marlene persisted, "Sheila, I really need you to do this."

"Marlene, you know I don't do things like that," I reasoned.

"I know that," she said, "but I'm stuck."

"Ask someone else," I said. "You know lots of women who are talented speakers. I've been a singer and a talk-show host, but I'm not a speaker—never have been, never will be. Thank you, and amen!"

"Okay," Marlene finally admitted, "here's the deal. I've already asked everybody else. You are the bottom of the barrel."

Honestly, that was the only reason I said I would do it. I mean, how high could the expectations be from the bottom of the barrel?

Then Saturday morning rolled around, and I was so mad at myself for agreeing to speak. Have you ever done that? You say yes to something, not really thinking it through, then suddenly it's upon you and you start praying for the imminent return of Christ.

I took a look at my sparse wardrobe and sighed. I'd left my five years' worth of on-air clothes behind me in Virginia Beach for the next cohost, and I had nothing suitable for a country club lunch in Palm Springs.

Finally settling on a pair of dress slacks and a silk blouse, I dressed and dragged my sorry self out to my car. It was about an hour's drive from my apartment to Palm Springs, and I complained to the Lord the entire trip: "I don't have anything to say! What do I have in common with these women? Why didn't you stop me? This is not going to make you look good, you know!"

Lord, This Is Not Funny!

As I pulled into the palm tree—lined driveway, I saw exquisitely dressed women relinquishing their car keys to young valets in red blazers.

"Good grief!" I said. "Lord, this is not funny. I have no idea what to do here!"

I heard in my heart, *I do. Follow me.*

I was received in the lobby by a very kind welcoming committee. I was sorely tempted to introduce myself with, "Hello. Some call me Sheila, but you may refer to me as the bottom of the barrel," but I didn't. After a delicious-looking lunch, which I was too nervous to touch, the chair-lady introduced me. She was obviously not aware of the "bottom of the barrel" thing. She talked about my years in broadcasting at the BBC in London, my books, my music, and my years as cohost of *The 700 Club*. I could feel the expectation level in the room rise in direct proportion to how low I was slipping in my chair.

13

I walked slowly to the platform with my heart thudding in my chest and climbed the five steps that took me to the podium. I closed my eyes for a moment, feeling two things: one, I felt unbearably inadequate; two, I was deeply aware of the presence of Christ. I heard him say to my heart, *Just tell the truth*. So I did.

I told that room full of ladies that just a few months before I had been in the locked ward of a psychiatric hospital. I told them that for years I tried to hide behind perfect makeup and hair. I told them that I had found that public Christian ministry is the perfect place to hide, because no one questions your motives or wonders if your drive to do more and more comes from a call or a wound, from passion or panic. I told them that I believed that when we are unwilling or unable to deal with the pain of life, we find a place to hide. It can be at the bottom of a bottle or a stranger's bed, a perfect home or a perfect face, but we are not free. I told them that I came to the place where the pain of staying the same was greater than the pain of change, whatever that might be. I told them that Jesus Christ had rescued me and that my life now was following him one step at a time.

Suddenly I became aware of how quiet the room was. No one clinked a spoon against a coffee cup or rummaged through a purse or jacket pocket for a cell phone. I looked out at the crowd and began to really search the faces. One woman in the front row had tears running down her cheeks. Farther back, a woman had her face in her hands.

I had no idea what to do. I didn't really understand what was going on. As far as I knew, my story was a reason for people to politely and kindly move away. Mostly, I thought that what I had gone through was just my story and no one else would be able to relate to it.

When I finished, I wasn't sure what I was supposed to do next.

This was the first time I had ever spoken to a group of women. So I just said, "Well, that's about it. I'm not in a hurry to get anywhere, so I'll just hang around in case anyone wants to talk."

When Brokenness Becomes a Bridge

One by one, women came up and began to tell me their stories. I was stunned by the transparency taking place. Through tears the women talked about addiction to alcohol and pills, affairs, depression, and anxiety. It was as if for a moment there was an understanding that it was all right to be human after all, to be broken, to be real and to talk about it.

I was shocked—not by what the women were saying but because I always thought that people wanted me to be perfect so I could help them. If I reached out for help myself, I had reasoned, then I would lose my perceived usefulness. Suddenly I began to see that my brokenness was a far greater bridge to others than my pretended wholeness had ever been.

As I reflect on that now, I can hardly believe that I once thought and lived as I had. There is a kind of perverted arrogance in the mentality of perfection. I didn't mean to be arrogant. I didn't understand that I had adopted a platform that only Christ can stand on. But the truth is, all I have to offer to anyone else is a life surrendered to Christ so that his beauty and grace shine through my brokenness. Those would have sounded like lovely lyrics to a worship song before, but now I know the truth of them and the freedom that comes from understanding—I am not the good news!

So I had muttered all the way to that luncheon, and then cried all the way home. "You knew it would be like this," I whispered to God, taking those few hours and tucking them in my heart.

Fast Forward

My heart was opening in other, new ways too. In December 1994, Barry and I were married, a beautiful wedding in St. Matthew's Lutheran Church in Charleston, South Carolina. As my family still lives in the United Kingdom, it made sense to be married where Barry's mom and dad lived.

After the wedding, we crossed the country again, back to the Pacific coast and Laguna Niguel, where we rented a home and settled into a peaceful first year of marriage. Barry was head of programming at a television network in Southern California, and I was still a student at Fuller Seminary. I had no idea what I would do when I graduated, but I was pretty sure I never wanted to be in the spotlight again in any way. I often reflected on that day in Palm Desert and saw it as a moment of grace splashed into the bottom of the barrel. I was deeply grateful to have been used by God in such an unexpected way that day, and I found myself opening more and more to wherever God might take me.

Almost every day I flicked through my Bible until I came to the passage in Isaiah to see if it still burned with the same intensity. It always did.

One morning I asked the Lord, "Is this something I need to do anything about?"

No, I heard in my heart. *Just follow me.*

Now It Springs Forth

Some time later I received a note in the mail from a friend asking me to sing at a small missions conference he was hosting in Anaheim, California. I wrote back, thanking him for his invitation, but told him that for the foreseeable future I was not doing any singing. I really believed that part of my life was over.

My friend persisted. He works with missionaries in so-called closed countries—those countries where you could lose your life or be imprisoned for sharing the gospel. In his follow-up letter he said he understood, but would I reconsider, as a favor for him?

As you may have gathered by now I am a total sucker for that.

I showed up that evening, and as far as I can remember all I did was sing a couple of songs.

Two weeks later I received a letter from a woman who works with her husband in an Islamic country. She wrote that on her long flight home God spoke to her about my life and gave her twelve things to tell me. Some of these twelve things made no sense to me at all, but as I read her letter I had a strong sense of the presence of God. I knew he was speaking to me. I finished reading on my knees.

For thirteen years I have carried this letter with me, sharing it only with Barry and my closest friends. Now I want to share it with you. As you read, please remember that these wonderful words came to me at a time in my life when I felt like such a failure in so many ways. I believed I had let down the Lord and his people; I was looking to the future with no sense that I would ever be able to serve the Lord again through song or word. Many of my friends still struggled then with the fact that I took medicine for depression. I was not in a strong place. I was in a quiet place, tucked away from the life I used to live. Into this broken heart God spoke words that made me sob out loud as I read them:

Dear Sheila,

On Saturday night, March 5, 1996, as you were ministering to us through songs, the Lord gave me the following words of encouragement for you.

1. The beauty of the Lord is so strong and vibrant in you. His anointing and approval upon your life is very obvious.

2. The fragrance of God through your years of crushing smells wonderful. The fullness of His character in your character is so sound yet silent.

3. Years were spent with some people who may have been a thorn in your heart, but your confidence in God's love for you made your heart bigger and bigger and so easily moved for His people.

4. The Lord is preparing a table for you, a table of newness. There is a newness coming to your life. The Lord will give you new songs and a new uniform is being made for you. The period of boot camp is over and it is time for promotion.

5. A new book has opened in your life. A new verse has been written in your heart. A new fragrance is given to you and a new style. A new heart and new eyes. Suddenly you will be able to see life differently. You will see yourself a new person, changed for the glory, moved by his holiness, clothed in righteousness singing a message of freedom.

6. The Lord has guarded your heart throughout the years. Your heart in the hands of the King has been kept like a child in a mother's womb.

7. The Lord is saying, Come my child, I want to give you new roses without thorns. I will add to your fragrance without additional crushing. I will provide the comfort and peace you have been waiting for, for many years. Just concentrate on Proverbs 3, meditate on my words constantly, for out of the richness of my word in you, there shall flow waters of life into people's lives.

8. Watch out for distractions that may come your way, for the enemy wants to steal the necklace of turquoise that I

gave you years ago. Remain transparent and simple, for
the Lord is with simple-hearted people.

9. I have brought you to the still waters, says the Lord. Come,
   drink, and let your soul be satisfied with this new still-
   ness and get used to this new peace that I have brought to
   your life.

10. Your son has a special protection over him. The Lord will
    guard his heart as you guard your own heart. I will provide
    for him, says the Lord, I will protect and guard him.

11. I will bring new women in your life. You will be an instru-
    ment of love in their ears. There will be opportunities to
    minister to women globally. You will come out of this
    training as a Queen Esther.

12. Your ministry will bloom in victory in the coming years
    and your body will rejuvenate and be strong to do what
    the Lord has planned for your life.

I read this letter over and over, wanting to thank the woman
who wrote it. We had never met before, so she knew nothing of
my life, and there was no address on the envelope, just a signa-
ture inside. I've never been able to contact this woman to tell her
what her letter has meant and continues to mean to me. But she
was an obedient vessel in God's hands, though at the time many
things she said were a mystery to me.

The first mystery was what was shared in item four. The language seemed strange to me. "A new uniform is being made for
you. The period of boot camp is over and it is time for promotion." Those images seemed better suited to a man. I couldn't
figure out what this meant for me, so I put thoughts of it aside to
think about later.

Item ten caught my attention, seeming even more confusing: "Your son has a special protection over him."

My son?

We had no son. Barry and I had only been married for three months and I wasn't pregnant. I had no idea what this could mean and thought even the idea of me having a son could be far-fetched. At my age it was quite possible that I would be unable to conceive— something Barry and I had talked through before committing to marry.

Would we, at some point, adopt a son? I wondered.

At this point only God knew.

One Year Later

When I did get pregnant, Barry and I were so excited as we drove to our ultrasound appointment. We were pretty sure I was carrying a girl and had even chosen the name: Alexandra. When the technician told us that we were having a boy, Barry did some dance known only to men from the beginning of time. I was thrilled too. I loved the idea of having a son.

Our joy was short-lived however. The following week my doctor called to say that she was pretty sure something was wrong with our son. She asked if I would be willing to have an amniocentesis. Initially I said no. We would face whatever we had to when our baby was born.

The doctor pressed me to reconsider. Since you are forty, she said, it would help to know what we are dealing with now.

So I agreed.

I don't know if you have ever had this procedure, but I found it very difficult. Just one week before, I had been in the same office, on the same table, watching the screen with eagle eyes for the first glimpse of our baby. Now the nurse was scrutinizing the screen to make sure the long needle used to extract amniotic fluid did not harm him. Barry watched with tears running down his face.

Five days later our fears were confirmed. We were told that it appeared as if our child would be seriously handicapped.

What Kind of New Beginning Is This?

The following weeks and months were an emotional roller coaster. Some days I felt strong and full of hope, and others I was overwhelmed and afraid. It was clear to me that not every new beginning would be one I would have chosen. I had to dig deeper and deeper into God's Word and into my own heart and soul to find a place of rest. I wanted to know: what does trust look like here where the rubber absolutely meets the road?

I read and reread that letter from the woman who heard me sing the previous year, and was struck by the instruction to settle my heart in Proverbs 3. I have known verses 5 and 6 since I was a teenager:

> Trust in the Lord with all your heart
> and do not lean on your own understanding.
> In all your ways acknowledge Him,
> and He will make your paths straight. (NASB)

Words that had brought me so much comfort in the past now seemed elusive. What does it look like to put aside my understanding? I couldn't un-know what I knew.

I began to study as many Bible commentaries as I could get my hands on and found a lot of practical help. With fresh eyes I saw myself standing in the middle of a storm. The winds could increase and decrease in intensity, and I was being asked to trust

God, not pretend everything was fine. I needed to decide what I would lean on. I could choose to lean on what I understood from the doctor and my own thoughts, or I could choose to lean on Christ, who stood like a redwood tree, not bowing one way or the other with the wind.

This is how I would learn to trust: I would choose over and over to lean on him. The choice wasn't a one-time deal, but one that must be made every time a new wind threatened to blow me over. I began to ask God to show me how to acknowledge him in every area of my life. This meant what I chose to think about, how I spent my time and money, how I treated others. I consciously brought every area of my life before God and offered it to him again. I decided that nothing was too small or insignificant and invited the Holy Spirit to point to anything I needed to let go.

During the weeks and months of fetal monitoring, I would lean on God's promise that he would protect my baby. I didn't know what that would look like, but I tucked that promise into my heart. On my hardest days, with tears for this little one growing inside of me, I would picture myself leaning on Christ and being held by him.

Near the end of my pregnancy, my doctor called with more news.

She told me that on the day that the results from my amniocentesis came back, she had received results for another forty-year-old patient. That woman's results had been placed in my chart by mistake and mine in hers. There had never been anything wrong with our baby boy.

Even as the first wave of relief rolled over me, I stopped for a moment and realized that some woman I'd never met was getting a very different call. There was nothing I could do but pray that Christ would be with her as he was with me.

It was becoming much clearer to me that if I tried to rely on my understanding of what happened around me, I'd be in big trouble, because some things just make no sense at all. I knew that I could have walked through the previous six months consumed by anxiety for a situation that I had no control over. When I trusted in the Lord, however, I always found him there, strong, loving, trustworthy.

Learning to trust was changing my life—not in one grand swoop, but moment by moment.

Still, I had many questions and would wonder about things in that letter I'd received from the woman who heard me sing.

More Than Casseroles

One of the things that perplexed me was this woman's mention of "your ministry" and "there will be opportunities for you to minister to women globally."

Opportunities to minister to women seemed a far reality from where I have lived most of my life. In college my best friends were guys—I suppose because I could hang around with them and they wouldn't pry into my past or ask deep, emotional questions. For years after that I toured with an all-male band, so I had become used to living a fairly solitary life. I had a few female friends, like Marlene, but the thought of ministering to large groups of women intimidated me. I had an image of what that role would look like, and it seemed far better suited to the daughters of Billy Graham than to me. When I thought of the kind of woman who ministers to other women, I imagined she played tennis or golf and went to coffee, swapped recipes with her friends, and laughed a lot. I knew that I wouldn't fit in. The things I laughed at didn't seem funny to anyone else!

But when I was willing to take a closer look at why I felt so reactive to this potential call, I saw that I was afraid of the kind of intimacy and level of honesty it might require. I was still licking my wounds from feeling betrayed by friends. The surprising thing for me was that when I had taken time to listen to many of those friends and colleagues before leaving Virginia Beach, they told me that they didn't feel they knew me at all.

One woman I had worked with for the entire five years of my role as cohost said, "No one felt they knew you well enough to ask what was going on, so we just had to guess."

Part of my feeling alienated, clearly, was of my own choosing. But why? I didn't know, and this new journey was becoming very uncomfortable.

"I wish you would let some parts of my life just rest, Lord."

I know.

"It's hard feeling vulnerable."

I know.

"When does this journey end?"

Just follow me.

THREE

THE HUNGER TO BELONG

The Beauty of Transparency

Anxiety has its use, stimulating us to seek with keener longing for that peace which is complete and unassailable.

—SAINT AUGUSTINE OF HIPPO

The strength of the fatherless was crushed. Therefore snares are all around you, and sudden fear troubles you.

—JOB 22:9–10

When my son Christian was a little boy, one of his favorite things to do was to burst into a room shouting, "Ta-da!" at the top of his lungs. He took great delight in presenting himself, whether he was in his best clothes or just a diaper. It never occurred to him that we would be anything but thrilled to see him!

That picture is still vivid in my mind. Some of Christian's exuberance was his personality, but I wonder if every child comes into this world with a God-given "Ta-da!" inside. If that is true, what happens to squelch that joyful confidence and replace it with a need to hide?

For some, one single event can silence that shout; for others it seems to get washed away over the years with the drip, drip, drip of shame and self-doubt. For me, the need to understand why I feared being known became a brick wall that I needed to break through to move forward with all that God wanted for me.

What Am I So Afraid Of?

Today one of the most treasured gifts in my life is the close relationship I have with my dearest friends. Why, then, did I go so many years keeping at arm's length those who pressed in to know me? In particular, I wondered:

- What is it that I am afraid people might find out about me?
- Why do I keep people at a distance?
- Why do I assume that if I let people in they would be disappointed and leave?
- Why do I fear rejection so intensely that I remove myself from the equation before anyone else gets to "vote me off the island"?

Do these questions resonate with you? Do you ever feel that you don't belong? Do you believe that if people knew all about you they would reject you? Are there parts of your life you have buried deep inside you because you are ashamed of them?

One thing that continues to surprise me is the commonality of so many of our struggles. I still tend to assume that if I am dealing with a very negative emotion, I am the only one who feels that way.

That's just not true.

I saw that again recently at a Women of Faith conference. For the past thirteen years I have been part of a team of women who travel to arenas around the country about thirty weekends a year. On Friday night each weekend the speakers, musicians, and dramatists meet backstage for an hour after dinner to catch up and pray for one another. At one of our cities in the summer of 2008, I was having a hard time. I was tired and missing my husband and son. I felt bad that I wouldn't be able to see Christian's football game the next day and was running the "I'm a bad mother" tape in my head. It was one of those times when I felt very inadequate in every area. I felt stretched so thin, as if I had nothing of real value to offer. So that's what I said in my prayer: "Father, I feel so empty tonight. I don't feel as if I have anything to bring to you. Sometimes I don't even feel as if I belong here."

After our prayer, two of the team members who are my good friends told me they feel the same way so much of the time.

Now I have traveled and spoken with these two friends in Women of Faith conferences for almost twelve years. I see them as very gifted and gracious (and they are)—and underneath the surface they were facing the same doubts that at times haunted me. I was shocked.

Dr. Gripka's words came back to me that night: "Jesus hasn't come to get you through the pain of life; he has come to live in you through it."

I began to see that when we keep our fears and wounds in the dark night of solitude, they never have a chance to heal; but when we share our pain, we invite others to come out of their darkness into the light of Christ for healing and hope. It's true that fresh wounds have to be covered to protect them from infection; it's also true that if they are never exposed to the light and to fresh air, they can't heal.

I am finding that healing and hope come not only in facing what is true myself, but in letting others in on my secret fears so that they might be able to face theirs as well. I think of the apostle Paul's words to the church in Galatia, "Bear one another's burdens, and so fulfill the law of Christ" (Galatians 6:2).

A Powerful Illustration

During the month I spent in the hospital, I kept hearing the same thing about myself over and over from all those around me: I was difficult to know. I found that very confusing because I see myself as a friendly person.

When I told my counselor this, he explained that it's one thing to be friendly but quite another to be vulnerable and transparent and let others into the areas where you feel most fragile.

One morning in a craft class, we were each given a piece of clay and told to model something that resembled our lives. I had no idea what to do with this lump of clay; I have no gift for sculpting. But this wasn't about the quality of art so I kept playing around with the clay. Eventually I came up with something: a small figure with very long arms, standing inside a walled circle. The arms were long enough for the figure to reach out and touch others, but no one got inside the wall to reach and touch her.

I studied my model for a long time. *This fits well*, I realized, with my commitment as a child to always be useful to God so that he would love me.

As I moved on in this journey, following after the Shepherd, he began to peel back layer after layer, allowing me to see the places I had kept hidden in the dark. This was a very painful process, but I have come to understand how necessary it is. One of the often uncomfortable realities of life is that God has designed us to live in integrity and health and community, and the parts of our story that we bury will continue to deal with us until we deal with them. I discovered that when I invited my Father to show me what I was hiding, he was waiting to do just that.

Today I can identify why I felt the need to hide for so long. I will touch on it briefly here, and then we'll look at possible reasons you feel dead or numb inside.

The room is quiet now
And all the anger stilled
But deep inside the voices rage against this little girl
They tell her to be quiet
They tell her she's alone
They tell her no one understands the terror in her home
She sees his face
The face she loves
It's twisted now with rage
She's trapped with him
No place to run
It's life on center stage
And some nights when she gets to sleep
He creeps inside her head
And stalks her till she cannot breathe
No refuge in her bed
She wonders what she did

To make her daddy hate her so
She tries to be the best she can
She does all that she knows
She walks around on broken glass afraid to make a noise
And prays that God will send someone to hear her little voice

October 5, 1992

Seeking a Father's Love

I was very traumatized by a brain injury my father suffered and then his death when I was a child. (I have written about it in more depth in *Honestly* and more recently in *Let Go*.[1]) The brain injury caused my father's behavior to become erratic and confusing, but children at ages four and five don't have the skills to understand that an adult's behavior may have absolutely nothing to do with them. The natural thought process for a child is, *If my mom or dad is angry with me, and lashes out at me, then I've done something wrong. I must deserve it.* The adult, after all, is the trusted authority figure.

So my dad had no control over his behavior, and I came to all the wrong conclusions. When he appeared to hate me, a deep sense of shame filled my soul. *If my own dad thinks I am worthless, then I must be truly worthless. If I try harder to behave, to be a good girl, maybe I can temper my dad's moods.*

Of course none of this worked. When my father died a few months later, I was left with a world of unanswered questions.

You might reasonably think, *Why didn't you ask your mother?*

There are some questions that you just don't ask as a child because the answer might destroy what little you have left of yourself. For me, add the deep sense of loyalty I had to my father and my belief that I deserved his actions toward me.

So when I became a Christian at age eleven, I transferred my performance from my dad, who was now gone, to God, my new Father. I was committed to making him love me, but it never felt as if I did enough. All I knew was that I wanted him to love me enough to cover whatever it was my dad saw in me. My childlike logic was that if I worked hard enough for God, the good should outweigh the bad . . . only I always felt that the scales were tipped against me. Nothing I did seemed to touch the depth of worthlessness I felt. When a child believes that there is something at her very core that makes her unacceptable, she will do whatever it takes to hide.

What About You?

There are many different reasons we feel a sense of shame, but how we then behave seems very much the same. If we believe there is something deep inside of us that others would reject, we hold ourselves back or simply vote ourselves out of life. This can lead to depression, addictions, bitterness, and despair. This is not the life Christ died to give you! We become used to living as we have lived for so long that it can be hard at times to vocalize what we feel.

When I travel now on weekends to speak at Women of Faith conferences, I stand at the back of the arena in the shadows and look out at the crowd. Initially it can seem like a sea of faces, but after thirteen years of speaking at these conferences to almost five million women, I have learned our song. I know that behind smiles and makeup are women who despise themselves, who are consumed with anger, lost in despair, struggling with their faith, and caught up in addictions or affairs. We share a silent desperateness. We have learned to hide our struggles so well that sometimes even we forget they are there.

If only our stories showed up on the outside of our lives and we wore them like a piece of jewelry, we might find hope and healing sooner.

I'm grateful that God is our Redeemer, and he will do what it takes to show us what's true. Sometimes he uses an unexpected moment to show us how much we still hurt under all the layers of protection—a moment like I experienced recently thanks to Twitter.

The Wonderful World of Twitter

If you had asked me a year ago about Twitter, I would have had no idea what you were talking about. Now I am fully engaged. Twitter is a free online social messaging network that allows people to stay connected in real time through their phones or computers. You choose people whose messages and updates you want to follow, and they choose you too.

For example, as I write this chapter, I have more than two thousand people who follow my Twitter updates. The question that appears at the top of the Twitter page on your computer or phone screen is simple: "What are you doing?" You are provided space to type a 140-character answer. I might type in, "Off to school to pick up Christian," or "Listening to Steven Curtis Chapman's new CD." That nugget of information goes out to everyone who follows me. (I don't follow everyone who follows me—only about one hundred people who are friends and colleagues of mine. To follow more would be overwhelming.)

Twitter gets really exciting during football season. I am a huge football fan and support the Dallas Cowboys and the Tennessee Titans. Several of my friends scattered across the country are big football fans too, so during games we let our Twitter updates or "Tweets" fly:

Did you see that interception?!
Is the referee blind?
Don't lose heart; remember, we are a fourth-quarter team.

It is a commentary on our culture that something like Twitter caught on so fast and is used by so many. I think it's because we feel more disconnected in our generation than previous generations did. With families spread across different states—or as in my case, around the world—the simple online tool of Twitter pulls the world right back between your own four walls.

Of course, Twitter is not for everyone. This kind of online social networking either really appeals to you, or it seems ridiculous. I, for one, love it! I love knowing where my friends are and what they are doing. I like to picture Marilyn Meberg sitting at her desk writing or Patsy Clairmont sitting by a big fire drinking tea. I love to keep up with all the changes in Natalie Grant's twin girls, Gracie and Bella, through pictures she posts to Twitter, called Twitpics. Also, there are times when Twitter can be a tremendous tool for prayer. For instance, in January 2009, I loved joining Max Lucado in prayer as our nation inaugurated its forty-fourth president. More than two hundred thousand Christians connected that morning through Twitter.

Most of the time, the Twitter updates from my friends make me laugh; but recently, one shot through me as if I had been stabbed in the heart. My response to this sweet message was overwhelming and confusing, alerting me to something deeper going on inside me.

The Pain of the Past

This particular message came from Gail Hyatt. Gail and Mike Hyatt are my dear friends, and Mike is the president and CEO of

Thomas Nelson Publishers. I had been enjoying all of their Twitter updates about the upcoming marriage of their daughter Megan; the wedding day finally came and went as a marvelous success. The following morning, Gail sent out a message as she reflected on the wedding:

> Weepiest moment @ the wedding: Joel coming 2 meet Megan as Mike walked her 2 the front & Mike putting her hand in Joel's. Powerfully visual.[2]

As I read that sweet reflection by a proud mother and grateful wife, I sat down on the floor in my bedroom and tears poured down my cheeks. I had no idea what was going on with me, but I have learned over the past few years that when I react as strongly as that to something, the roots go very deep. I do a lot of my thinking when I walk, so I put leashes on Belle and Tink, our two Bichon dogs, and set off into the cold, blustery day.

"Lord, I don't know why Gail's update made me feel so overwhelmingly sad," I prayed.

I do, I heard the Lord respond in my heart.

"Why should such a lovely moment make me suddenly feel small and very alone?"

You are never alone.

"Sometimes I feel as if I am."

I know.

"When I feel that way, I want to run away and hide."

Just trust me.

The Overwhelming Hunger to Belong

As I prayed and reread Gail's Twitter update about Megan's wedding, God began to speak to me and show me the truth about my reaction. In my mind as I pictured Joel coming to meet his bride. I saw Mike take Megan's hand and place it in Joel's. I thought how Mike and Gail had raised this lovely young woman, and now they were entrusting her to a man they knew and loved, believing in how he would tenderly care for her.

My heart ached as I realized, *I have never felt as if I really belong.*

That last word rang out inside me again and again: *Belonging. Belonging. Belonging.*

I sat with this realization for a while. I looked at what is true in my life today, and thought about all that I have: a loving husband, Barry, with whom I delight in our son, Christian. Certainly I have belonging with them, so much, and yet . . . the pain I was experiencing and the words attached to it were real.

I thought longer on the source of the pain and recognized it was from an old wound, something I'd harbored a long time.

Now old wounds don't just go away if we ignore them. Old wounds remember. We can bury them for a while, but at some point they will resurface until we deal with them; when the wound is from childhood, it can have very powerful emotion and logic attached to it, even if it is the distorted logic of a child's perspective.

Have you ever experienced this? Maybe you have listened to a song or watched a scene in a movie and suddenly you are overwhelmed by feelings out of proportion to what is happening around you? I believe that moments like these, although painful, are gifts to show us the parts of our heart that are still broken— and so that we can bring them to Christ for healing. These broken parts were buried a long time ago, and we have attempted to keep them contained in some internal tomb.

When I examine my response to Gail's sweet reflection, there seems to be a disconnect. What I felt that morning as I read her note was a deep ache that I have known since childhood, the ache to be loved and treasured and to belong. But my behavior belies that desire. Surely if I wanted to be loved, I wouldn't choose to live in such a defensive way. Yet emotions are far from logical, and wounds have their own set of rules. If your wounds tell you that you don't belong, you will rarely reach out for help—you fear too much being rejected again, and this time the wound will only go deeper.

To Belong

I have come to believe over the last few months that one of the greatest cries of the human heart is to belong. We want to know that if we didn't show up, we would be missed.

It's interesting that in the account of creation in Genesis, the first thing that God said was *not* good was that Adam was alone: "It's not good for the Man to be alone; I'll make him a helper, a companion" (Genesis 2:18 MSG). Humanity's deepest need was met, and Adam and Eve were one flesh. The tragedy is that if you read on through Genesis, chapter 3, once Adam and Eve sinned, that unity was gone and they hid from God. Adam and Eve lost that precious gift of a union previously known only by the Trinity. We lost it as well.

There is something inside of us that was made for knowing and being known; but once sin, fear, and insecurity entered the picture, the stakes became very high. When we get hurt, we back away and cover our wounds. Just like Adam and Eve, we hide. We do a pretty good job too.

Take Another Look

Imagine for a moment a beautiful church building. It is a traditional structure, and sunlight spills through the stained-glass windows. The church is full, the choir is singing a closing song, and the pastor looks down at his notes, critically reflecting on the effectiveness of his message. He sighs from a place deep inside of him. You scan the congregation. There are people here of all shapes and sizes, all ages. Some people appear to be listening to the choir; one or two are rustling in purses looking for a cough drop, car keys, a tissue. One man is fast asleep. A child is crawling under his father's legs, chasing an escaped toy.

Suddenly it's as if the lighting changes and the whole scene shifts.

Instead of seeing what's on the outside of each man, woman, and child, you see the burdens they are carrying. You see the wounds and scars they try so hard to hide. You see the truth, and it is shocking. You are even more alarmed when you realize the service is over and everyone intends to leave like that.

Part of you wants to cry out, "Don't leave yet! Don't take those burdens home with you! Stay for a while and let Jesus heal those wounded places."

But no one can hear you. Soon, everyone is gone.

I think this happens every Sunday in churches across this nation. We don't get to see that picture, but God sees it every moment of every day. I think part of the problem is that we have forgotten there is a better way to live. Some of our wounds are so deep that they are simply part of us now.

An Offer

Now revisit that church. The choir has finished. As the singers turn to leave the platform they hear a voice speaking. It's not their pastor's voice, which at times can waver with the twists and turns of life. This is a strong, passionate voice with a simple offer.

"If anyone thirsts, let him come to me and drink. Rivers of living water will brim and spill out of the depths of anyone who believes in me this way" (John 7:37–38 MSG).

The words ring out, but no one moves toward the speaker. Instead, the people grab their purses and jackets, their Bibles and choir books and turn to leave the building as usual.

Even as you watch, you can't believe what you see. You want to say, "Do you know who this is? Why don't you run to the front and throw yourself at his feet?"

Let's face it, this happens every day, every week. It happens to you and to me. So why don't we run to the front and fall at the feet of Jesus? Why do we resist Jesus' call to live—to really live? I think our lives have taught us that no one is coming to rescue us, so we stop dreaming.

Christ's offer is breathtaking to those who acknowledge that they are thirsty, for it is more pure and satisfying than anything we can find on this planet. Think about what Jesus offers: "If *anyone* thirsts, let him come to me." This is not an offer made only to those who have their act together, whose children are model students, and whose husbands know how to load the dishwasher. It's not an exclusive offer to those who have made good choices up until this very moment. It is an invitation to anyone who has finally come to the place where they are tired of pretending that everything is fine. It is an offer made to you and to me.

It's scary to come out of hiding if you have lived that way for years, but it's lonely to stay that way too. God knows everything about you and loves you. Will you trust him with your past and follow him?

If you say yes, you take a risk. What if you decide that you want to trust God with everything that is in you, and nothing happens? What if there is no bolt of lightning or page suddenly illuminated in Scripture with clear directions to follow? What if you are willing, but you are stuck waiting?

This is where I met the first friend on my path to trust, a friend who had a lot to say to me. Her name is Anna.

FOUR

A Broken Dream Becomes a Beautiful Life

The Beauty of Waiting and Being Present

No man ever sank under the burden of the day. It is when tomorrow's burden is added to the burden of today that the weight is more than a man can bear. Never load yourself so. If you find yourself so loaded, at least remember this: it is your own doing, not God's. He begs you to leave the future to him, and mind the present.

—George MacDonald

Anna the prophetess was also there, a daughter of Phanuel from the tribe of Asher. She was by now a very old woman. She had been married seven years and a widow for eighty-four. She never left the Temple area, worshiping night and day with her fastings and prayers. At the very time Simeon was praying, she showed up, broke into an anthem of praise to God, and talked about the child to all who were waiting expectantly for the freeing of Jerusalem.

—Luke 2:36–38 MSG

One of the toughest lessons for my son to learn is patience. If Christian can't master something in less than ten minutes, then he considers himself a failure. I've tried to help him understand that very few people come into this world intuitively skilled in any discipline. Most people, even those who have a gift, work hard at developing that gift or fine-tuning it. He seems unconvinced or at least unimpressed.

My son's first venture into the practice of patience and showing up came with the wide world of sports—and soccer.

Now I grew up in Scotland, a nation passionate about soccer. I love the game, though maybe not as much as Kenny Dalglish, one of Scotland's greatest soccer players. Dalglish was asked in an interview, "Do you think that soccer is becoming like a religion in Scotland?" He replied, "Oh no, it's much more important than that."

So when Christian's first soccer team met I was excited about everything: the game, the goals, and his teammates, which included an interesting bunch of boys. Some were there because they loved the game and had previous experience. Others, like Christian, were new to soccer but keen to learn. One or two were there because their dads thought they ought to play. One boy, in particular, spent most of his time on the field digging holes in the grass and collecting worms . . . not a familiar soccer position to me.

Clearly, this boy and a few others had neither the desire nor skill for the game.

Barry and I sat on the sidelines at the first practice with the other parents in our chairs from Dick's Sporting Goods. I thought the practice went well, and even the worm collector didn't come up empty-handed.

But when Christian got into the car, his first words were, "I quit."

I asked him why he felt that way.

"Because I stink!"

"Sweet pea," I soothed, "this was your first practice, what did you expect to be able to do?"

"I expected to be able to play soccer," he said.

"Christian, you have to learn, and that takes time."

Christian considered this. "Well, that's annoying," he replied.

Since then, Christian has persevered—and become a good soccer player.

Then football season began.

Christian's frustration with himself grew even worse. Could you blame him? American football is a challenging game for many reasons. The first time I saw my little boy in his massive shoulder pads and helmet, I didn't know whether to laugh or cry. It terrified me to think of gigantic lumps of budding masculinity hurling themselves at him, even if he was wrapped up like Darth Vader.

Barry's advice to Christian was, "If you see a big guy coming for you, go low and bring him down."

My advice: "If you see a big guy coming for you, run and hide in a bush."

And within no time at all Christian was convinced that no boy had ever been a worse football player than he. After the first game, he wanted to quit; but his dad and I said no, he had to give playing a fair shot.

It took him most of the first season to come to a place of believing that he was actually learning something. The first time he really tackled a boy and brought him down, he was over the moon. "Did you see me, Mom? I dived, I twisted, and I smashed him to the ground!"

Wow, I thought. *Isn't that just what every mother wants to hear?*

Then came basketball. I'm sure by now you can detect the

pattern. After one disappointing game where Christian's team suffered a significant loss, he decided that he was done with basketball.

I asked him to try to work out what he was feeling inside—why did he want to quit? Was he embarrassed? Did he dislike the game?

After some thought, he said, "I just don't think I'll ever be good enough, so why keep trying? Think about it, Mom: I'm never going to be Michael Jordan."

I told him that I agreed with his last statement but not his first, and then I told him a few things he didn't know:

- Michael Jordan was cut from his high school basketball team.
- Twenty-three publishers turned down Dr. Seuss's first book. The twenty-fourth company took it and sold six million copies.
- In their first year of business, the Coca-Cola Company sold only four hundred Cokes.
- A twenty-eight-year-old poet had his poems returned from the *Atlantic Monthly*, as they had no place for that kind of verse. I am very grateful that Robert Frost did not give up.
- Johnny loved football and wanted to play for Notre Dame; but he was told he was too small, so he played for a smaller college. As a ninth-round draft pick, he was signed to the Pittsburgh Steelers, but they cut him so he worked as a construction worker. He kept trying until the Baltimore Colts finally signed him. In 1957, Johnny Unitas was named the NFL's most valuable player and the following year he led the Colts to a win in the NFL championships.[1]

When you hear about people like this, who pursue a dream or vision that God has given them, do you wonder if they are simply born with a tenacity that is greater than most? Perhaps you find yourself in a place even now where you are waiting to see something happen that you believe God promised to you years ago.

What do you do in the waiting years? How do you trust God when there are no physical signs to encourage you? Are you tempted to put your life on hold as you wait, not committing to anything or anyone else in case you miss your moment?

I don't think God wants us to take a timeout or give up. I think we are asked to get into the game of life, to live each day as if it is the only day we will live by his grace. If God has planted a dream or vision in us, we will not miss it. That dream will unfold in his perfect way and in his perfect time if we are waiting, ready, and watching—and I don't think any woman in the Bible demonstrates that more beautifully than the prophetess Anna.

A Broken Dream

Anna's story begins with a hard twist in the road. We meet her in Luke 2:36–37, when she is old and poor and alone.

We learn that she has been a widow for most of her life and was married just seven years when her husband died. Since it was common for girls in Anna's day to be married by age thirteen, and she has been a widow for eighty-four years (or was now eighty-four years old), it's surmised that her husband died when she was around age twenty.

Imagine being so young, looking forward to making a home and growing a family, and then everything changes. No more dreams of having children or growing old with your husband. No hope of a beautiful home. No livelihood.

In Anna's day, there was no financial provision from the

government and unless a family offered support, widows were almost guaranteed a life of poverty. Even the apostle Paul addresses the sadness of this in his first letter to Timothy, advising young widows to remarry so that they would not be left wandering from home to home trying to find a place to belong and potentially lose their way (1 Timothy 5:13–14).

How easy it would have been for Anna to say, "This stinks. I expected to be a wife and mother. I expected to have a home. All the rules seem to be changing. I quit!"

But Anna, Luke tells us, was a prophetess, and she never left the temple.

When Luke calls Anna a prophetess, he is telling us that she had a special role speaking for the Lord. In all the Old Testament only five women are identified as prophetesses: Miriam, Moses's sister who led all the women of Israel in a song of praise after their escape from Egypt. Deborah, the only female among the judges who ruled with the heart of a mother over Israel before they had a king (Judges 5:7). And then three others whom we know little about: Huldah, Nodiah (named a false prophetess), and Isaiah's wife.

Did Anna sing, like Miriam, praises of God's goodness? Did she speak like Deborah with the heart of a mother?

We do know Anna dedicated her whole life to immersing herself in the Word of God and in his presence and sharing his Word with other women who came to the temple. She stayed in the game when it came to faith—even if life might have whispered: *Do you really have the desire for this? Do you think, as a poor, single widow you have the skills to encourage other women to love the Lord?*

Those whispers were there, you see, because Anna came from the tribe of Asher (Luke 2:36), a group of people who had turned their backs on God.

Who Am I?

Do you ever look at your family, at where you have come from, and doubt that God could ever use you? *Why would he put me in the game?* you might wonder, like a certain soccer player digging for worms on the sidelines. *I don't have the experience or the skills. I don't even know if I have the desire.* And what if you didn't even have parents who loved the game?

Anna could have chosen to think this since her ancestors were of the tribe of Asher, one of ten that had split from the kingdom of Israel after Solomon's reign and moved to the north. Imagine their departure, after witnessing all the miracles of God in their lives: the escape out of Egypt from Pharaoh, the parting of the Red Sea, the issuing of the Ten Commandments, the blessing of manna every morning, the battles won, the rise of a king, the building of the temple. All this, and still they had no more trust in God.

So the northern ten tribes, Israel, rebelled against God and refused to acknowledge the grandson of David as God's chosen king, appointing instead their own line of corrupt kings. Meanwhile, the southern two tribes, Judah, remained true to God's ways.

In the Northern Kingdom, there was a remnant of people who still honored God and went to worship in the city of Jerusalem seven times a year to celebrate the feasts. Jerusalem was in the Southern Kingdom, and according to the Law, the only place where God's priests could offer sacrifices. The journey by this remnant of believers, however, cost them everything they had— they had to leave their land and all their possessions behind.

How hard that must have been. How difficult to give up your home and expectations, to choose poverty and pain in order to worship God and look for the Messiah.

The people waited a long time. Seven hundred years before the birth of Christ, the ten tribes in the north were captured and taken into slavery in a foreign nation. Very few ever came home again.

But God's grace has no limits, not with time or distance.

So when Anna's family returned to Jerusalem from the tribe of Asher, they left all they had to worship God; like the rest of the faithful, they sought the new Messiah, the King who again would free them from slavery and poverty. And God, known to hang out with those on the sidelines, chose one from among them who had lost even more—Anna, the poor, single, aged widow—to see the Messiah with her own eyes.

A God-Ordained Moment

Scripture says that Anna never left the temple. That might sound strange if you are trying to imagine a woman camping out in your church facility for eighty-four years. However, there were apartments in the temple courtyard (Luke 2:36–38); Anna was such a godly woman that she had been allowed to stay in one of these small rooms. Ever waiting, ever watching, she served God there day and night; in the temple she fasted, prayed, and shared God's Word with other women.

I think about her praying faithfully for all those years, how she must have petitioned God for the Messiah to come. But did she ever imagine she would be one of two people in the temple one day to see the newborn Jesus face to face?

When Jesus was eight days old, his mother and father brought him to the temple in Jerusalem. According to Jewish custom, Jesus was to be presented and offered to God for his blessing and to make the required sacrifice.

But thousands of people were in and out of the temple all the time, and it was a massive structure. Built by the exiles who had returned from Babylon, the temple was then rebuilt by Herod the Great, king of Judea, as a way to try to improve his relationship with the vast population of Jews living in Judea. The work began eighteen years before Christ was born and continued for sixty-five years after Christ's birth.

How could anyone have even planned to be in the right spot at the right time to see Jesus?

Simeon may not have planned the particulars of that encounter, but like Anna, he waited and prayed for it all his life. He was a godly man who had been told by God that he would not die until he had seen the Messiah with his own eyes. When Mary and Joseph entered the temple, Simeon saw their child and immediately recognized him as the Messiah. Simeon took into his arms baby Jesus, proclaiming a beautiful benediction and blessing:

> Lord, now You are letting Your servant depart in peace,
> According to Your word;
> For my eyes have seen Your salvation
> Which You have prepared before the face of all peoples,
> A light to bring revelation to the Gentiles,
> And the glory of Your people Israel. (Luke 2:29–32)

And just at this moment, in walks Anna. The poor, aged widow, who all her life gave much and got little—the amazing woman who trusted by waiting and watching, is blessed in her life and for all time.

Are You Watching?

I find an interesting parallel between Anna's life and our lives today.

Then, every loyal Jew was expecting Christ, but almost no one recognized him when he came. The people were troubled, oppressed, taxed, persecuted, and looking for a different kind of Messiah—one who arrived in physical power to build an earthly kingdom, not one born in a stable to save us from our sins.

Today we are to be watching and waiting for Christ's return, and we also live in trying times. Many people are losing their financial security every day. Too many of our days can be eaten up with worry and stress or we can follow after the Shepherd, trusting him to watch over us and walk beside us.

Anna shows us that we don't have to know all the particulars, that we can feel like our lives are on the sidelines, and yet God is still at work. He uses even the ones who wait and watch and simply show up. The fact that Anna was allowed to take up residence in the temple courts tells us a lot about the kind of woman God loves. Day in and day out she faithfully did what mattered above all else: fasting, praying, and speaking his Word. Her life became a thing of beauty and grace, transformed by a heart that trusted God.

Waiting, of course, is never easy. Sometimes it's not only hard but devastating. When I hit that obstacle, I remember a man and his two sisters who have quite a story to tell about what it feels like when you call on God and he doesn't seem to show up.

FIVE

WHY THE PAIN?

The Beauty of Crying Out to Jesus

Why is it that we rejoice at a birth and grieve at a funeral?
It is because we are not the person involved.

—MARK TWAIN

When Jesus saw her sobbing and the Jews with her sobbing,
a deep anger welled up within him. He said, "Where did you
put him?"

—JOHN 11:33–34 MSG

Life is full of moments. Some make us laugh till tears run down our cheeks. Some take our breath away; others have the potential to change the course of our lives. I have the priceless gift of being in the company of those who make me laugh until I can hardly breathe. I am a firm believer in the therapeutic benefits of throwing your head back and laughing from the deepest place inside you. It may not change your circumstances, but it's like a vitamin shot to your spirit. For me, it places the confidence to say, "I can do this" back into a difficult challenge or a dark night.

When Eleanor, my mother-in-law, was in the last days of her battle with liver cancer, there were moments of humor that made this difficult transition more bearable. One night after I had given her some liquid morphine in ginger ale to help ease her pain, she pointed at her husband, William, and asked me, "Is that my husband?"

I assured her that he was indeed her faithful companion of many years.

Her ensuing look of disgust as she plopped back down onto the pillow had William and me in hysterics.

William and Eleanor had many challenging moments in their marriage, yet they found a way to make it work for them. One of William's greatest survival tools when Eleanor got upset was his fascinating friendship with a number of cats over the years. Whenever Eleanor wanted to discuss something controversial (like their new pastor) or was mad about something (like their new pastor), William's classic response was, "Look at Cinder!" (or whatever the name of the current cat).

The first time I experienced this dynamic for myself was when I was sitting at the breakfast table with them drinking coffee and Eleanor was attempting to give me fifty-three good reasons why I should not marry her son. I was quite stunned by the speech.

Finally Eleanor turned to William and said, "Well, add something!"

William's pièce de résistance was, "Look at Cinder!"

I turned to look at the cat, expecting something fairly theatrical if it demanded more attention than Eleanor's speech. But Cinder was just sitting on a chair being a cat. He wasn't knitting or reading *War and Peace*; he wasn't texting a message on a cell phone or selling stock. No, he was just licking his fur and being a cat.

I enjoyed many more than my fair share of hilarious moments with William, but I think the funniest was the night he thought God was going to heal Eleanor.

Tell Me That God's Not Healing Her!

At one point during Eleanor's cancer struggle, I had asked if there was anything I could do to make her days more full of meaning and joy.

She asked me if I thought it possible for Lana Bateman, our Women of Faith intercessor, to fly in and pray with her. Lana is such a peaceful person to be around that I wasn't surprised that Eleanor, in her last days on earth, longed for Lana's company.

I called Lana and we set up her flights. Then she began a vigil of sitting by Eleanor's bed, playing a beautiful worship CD, and softly praying for her.

One evening, William and I were in the kitchen fixing supper and Lana came down for something to drink. As she turned to go back upstairs she said to us, "Eleanor seems stronger tonight."

I looked at William, who had an expression of pure horror on his face.

"Pop," I asked, "are you all right?"

He looked at me for a moment and said, "Please tell me that God's not healing her!"

I laughed so hard I nearly burst a kidney.

I realize this story may be hard for some people to understand, but if you had lived through the years of "discussions" and ups and downs in William and Eleanor's marriage, his comment had a certain flair to it. I think it might even have put a smile on God's face!

Each of us has moments in life that make us laugh out loud or sober our spirits. We walk long paths with certain people, full of "discussion," hard knocks, and sheer joy too. Along the way, at certain moments, we might be called to sit for long vigils at the side of disappointment and grief. We might doubt everything we've come to believe about the goodness of God and his care for us. We might be searching for the rhyme and reason of it all.

Siblings Mary, Martha, and Lazarus of the New Testament had such a long journey. When their brother became deathly ill, the sisters faced a bitter vigil at his side. They cried for help, someone to join them beside Lazarus, to reassure them that he would get better, that he would not die—at least not yet. They trusted their friend Jesus, who had been rounding the countryside healing strangers, to come to them and save their brother too.

But when Jesus stayed away, though not far from them, the sisters must have searched for *why*. Imagine the breach of trust they felt. Imagine their heartbreak, shock, and amazement when Jesus does arrive, long after their brother has died, and the Lord weeps.

Why doesn't he do something? they must have wondered.

Then he does, and that mystifies them more. *Look*, he had been saying all along. *Look at Lazarus*.

The Unbelievable and the Unthinkable

Now we don't know how Mary, Martha, and Lazarus became so close to Jesus. In fact, we don't know much about the siblings at all, not their ages, or if they ever married and lost a spouse so that they needed to live together as adults. But Scripture does tell us that Jesus stayed with them in their home from time to time (Luke 10:38), and counted them dear friends. In fact, John 11:5 says, "Jesus loved Martha and her sister and Lazarus."

It's interesting that Scripture names Martha first in this list of who Jesus loved. So often Martha gets maligned for being the pragmatic one, always about busyness, maybe missing the point. Remember how when Jesus came to visit, Martha attempted to make sure the event was properly catered, while Mary sat at Jesus' feet and drank in every word, even when her sister fussed at her? So maybe Martha missed the point there, but this reference also suggests that Martha was the one who held everything together (perhaps she was the eldest of the three), and I imagine Mary (maybe the youngest) was the dreamer.

So when their brother becomes gravely ill, I can see Mary sitting beside him, sponging his brow, whispering in his ear as he is losing ground moment by moment. "Jesus will be here, Lazarus. Just hold on. I know he'll be here soon." Mary completely trusts in that. Jesus is a friend, and Lazarus's name, after all, means "One whom God helps" (a bit of an understatement considering the rest of his story).

I can see Martha bustling around, working to get Jesus to them, sending messages, keeping the communications going. Maybe someone said to Martha: "Jesus is a very busy man. Lots of people want a piece of his time. What makes you think he'll drop whatever he is doing and come here?"

Martha, no less trusting of Jesus than her sister Mary, might have replied, "I'm sure he's on his way. He's our friend. Lazarus is like his own brother. Jesus will know that if we ask him to come, it must be very important. Trust me, he'll be here."

Abandoned

Only Jesus doesn't come. Mary and Martha have sent word to him from their home in Bethany, John 11:3 tells us.

"He whom you love is sick," their message reads.

Jesus is across the River Jordan, about twenty miles from them. It's at least a good day's walk, so the sisters must have expected him to arrive the following evening.

But the evening comes and goes and, still, Jesus has not come.

Lazarus languishes. His breathing becomes labored. The death rattle begins.

Were Mary and Martha both with Lazarus when he took his final breath, or was Martha outside scanning the horizon, looking for Jesus? Can you imagine Mary holding her brother's face and placing one hand on his heart, feeling for the beat, but instead feeling a cold, still shell? Or Martha, standing at the edge of their property, desperate to see Jesus walk toward her, sensing a sudden rush, the spirit of her brother leaving his body?

The moment must have been so sad, confusing, and devastating. Where was Jesus? Why was this happening when he loved them so?

The sisters felt so alone. Lazarus was gone now. They must have not only grieved the brother they loved, but feared for their future. The reality was they were two single women in a culture where men controlled the purse strings and even within the tabernacle all expression and connection to church leadership. Mary and Martha now had no man to look out for them or protect them; the one man they had counted on, more than any other, had let them down.

The sisters' thoughts must have fixed on certain questions, the kind that erode trust and repeat over and again in the mind when you feel abandoned: *Why hasn't Jesus come? Has something terrible happened? Why hasn't he even sent word? Does he no longer care? Has he no real control anyway? Why?*

Have you ever been there, prayed that God would let you in on what he's doing so life doesn't feel so out of control, but he is silent? Has it seemed he is busy helping others, maybe even those who don't believe, and he's withdrawn from you? Maybe you understand his love for the lost—you love them too. So you don't want him to change his plans. You just want to know that there is one. Yet you hear nothing.

Just a Stone's Throw Away

Across the Jordan River, just twenty miles or so from Bethany, Jesus is with his disciples, ministering to the people. They have retreated to this place because some of the Jewish leaders have become so hostile toward Jesus that he is in danger of being stoned to death; they are on the watch for him.

No wonder Jesus has their attention. He has been going around the country performing all sorts of miracles. The gospel of John recounts seven miracles in the three years of Jesus' public ministry: turning water into wine at the wedding in Cana, healing the sick and lame at the pool in Bethsaida, feeding a multitude of five thousand in the countryside with just two fishes and five barley loaves, walking on water in a stormy sea, giving a blind man sight, and in two instances bringing the dead back to life.

Luke 7 gives more detail about these resurrections—first about the centurion's servant who is sick. Jesus is willing to go to the soldier's house and bring his servant back to life. But the centurion, completely trusting, sends word: "Lord, do not trouble yourself, for I am not worthy to have you come under my roof. Therefore I did not presume to come to you. But say the word, and let my servant be healed" (Luke 7:6–7 ESV).

Jesus, amazed at the level of this man's faith, heals the servant without ever having to see him face to face.

Then Jesus crosses paths with a grieving mother on a funeral march. This mother is a widow who, some time earlier, buried her husband. Now she is on her way to bury her only child. Jesus touches the wooden frame carrying her son's casket and tells the dead boy to sit up—and the child does.

Not just the bystanders but even Jesus' own disciples marvel: two people brought back to life shortly after their deaths is stunning, remarkable—unimaginable—had they not seen with their own eyes. Seeing is believing for these witnesses. Jesus is the Great Physician, he is their Savior. It's easy to trust when you can see results.

Yet, amazing and miraculous as these restorations are, nothing prepares them for what is about to happen with Lazarus, for in the Jewish mind-set, there's a huge difference between the just-dead body and one dead for more than one day.

By the time Jesus gets to Bethany, Lazarus will have been dead four days.

We'll Just Die with You Then

The reality is Lazarus was probably dead by the time Jesus first heard that his friend was even sick. It would have taken one day for Mary and Martha's message to reach Jesus, and then he didn't exactly respond promptly. In fact:

> When Jesus heard that, He said, "This sickness is not unto death, but for the glory of God, that the Son of God may be glorified through it." Now Jesus loved Martha and her sister and Lazarus. So, when He heard that he was sick, He stayed two more days in the place where He was. (John 11:4–6)

How strange. Jesus hears his friends are in distress and he loves them . . . so he decides to stay right where he is, not coming to their call, not hurrying to offer his help. He knows it's taken one day for Mary and Martha's message to reach him, and he lingers where he is two days more, even knowing it will take him another day if he were to journey back.

The disciples are relieved for this decision, since returning to Judea could only mean trouble.

But after two days, when Jesus announces that he's ready now to cross the Jordan and go back to Bethany, they are horrified. *Have you forgotten*, they remind him, *that just a few days ago the people there tried to stone you?*

Jesus responds curiously. He says:

> Are there not twelve hours of daylight? Anyone who walks in daylight doesn't stumble because there's plenty of light from the sun. Walking at night, he might very well stumble because he can't see where he's going. (John 11:9–10 MSG)

And then he announces that Lazarus has "fallen asleep" and "I'm going to wake him up."

The disciples, of course, are thinking literally. They begin to rationalize among themselves. Why should they risk going back when they had just got away in time? Are they really needed anyway? Didn't Jesus say that Lazarus was simply asleep and would not die? They suppose Lazarus must have recovered from a bad fever or something.

Jesus corrects them, and he's explicit. "Lazarus died. And I am glad for your sakes that I wasn't there. You're about to be given new grounds for believing. Now let's go to him" (John 11:14–15 MSG).

To which Thomas, the disciple so many of us know today as "Doubting Thomas," says to his companions, "Come along. We might as well die with him" (John 11:16 MSG).

Doubting Thomas? I've often thought it's a bad rap that we've given Thomas, calling him this. Here, he shows me so. The disciple who later refuses to believe Christ has risen from the dead, unless he can see for himself the scarred hands, feet, and side of Jesus (John 20:25), shows us here remarkable loyalty, devotion, and trust. He has no certainty of the immediate outcome, and knows he cannot take Christ's place, so he pledges: *If Jesus is going there, I'm going with him*.

Perhaps Thomas's utterance of disbelief in the Upper Room was not out of cynicism and complete disbelief, but out of the haze of grief and despair. How might an encouraging word have changed things? Would we know this disciple as Trusting Thomas, if he had made in the Upper Room a rallying cry as he made here in John 11? And how was it the other disciples missed what Jesus was saying about following him and walking in the light?

George R. Beasley-Murray explains in a commentary on John's gospel:

One can walk in the day without stumbling, because one is aware of the light of this world [the sun] shining on one's path.

This is true of people generally and of Jesus in particular. He must walk in the [limited] time appointed for him; while he does so he knows he will not "stumble" for he is under the protection of God . . . the application . . . is the necessity of the disciple to keep in his company even though he does advance toward danger and death.[1]

This is not a thought to rush over or take lightly. For me, this has become a daily prayer. Each morning I say like Trusting Thomas, "Lord, I don't know where you are going today, but wherever it is, I'm coming with you." I decide I'm going to take the long journey with Jesus, whether that means walking through "discussions" and hard knocks, or into sheer joy because I have learned that the safest place to be is wherever Jesus is. Where he is may not always look the safest, but if it's where Jesus is, then that is where I want to be. Also, when uncertainty nips at my heels, as surely it did the disciples' that day Jesus led them back to Bethany, I think of another time they followed Jesus.

They were in a boat on the lake in the middle of a terrible storm while Jesus slept in the bow like a baby (Luke 8:22–25). The shore must have looked like the safest place to be, and from the tempestuous waters they cried out in fear. It's at that moment of despair that Jesus rose and spoke and even the sea obeyed him and calmed. Then the sea (or was it Jesus?) carried them safely to the other shore.

Of course, Jesus does not always lead us into safe, calm, and pleasant places, and he doesn't always give us signs and wonders at the very moment we cry out in despair. As Beasley-Murray says, he advances us toward death, but he is always in control, ever-watching, good, and always has a plan—and the disciples, Mary, and Martha are about to see this firsthand.

Where Were You?

By the time Jesus and the disciples reach the outskirts of Bethany, Lazarus has been in the tomb, and in the hot Palestinian climate, his body has begun to decay.

Mary and Martha must have lost hope of a miracle with each passing day. They knew of how Jesus had resurrected the centurion's servant and widow's son, restoring each of them almost immediately after death, certainly within hours.

Lazarus has been dead now for four days. According to Jewish tradition and custom his body has been coated in spices (the Hebrews did not embalm like the Egyptians), committed to its final resting place and placed in a tomb, and grave watchers must have seen and smelled Death.

The Jews, you see, believed that for three days the soul might return to the grave, thinking that it would reenter the body; but on day four it sees that the color of its face has changed and leaves for good. So there are people watching the grave. They are watching too because, according to custom, a body must be buried on the day of death, and there had been a few cases where the person buried was not dead but in a coma. So once the body had been committed to its final resting place, it was checked on for three days; after three days all hope of recovery was gone.[2]

No one had ever seen a body come out of the tomb on the fourth day; there was no doubt to anyone that Lazarus was dead.

So when Martha hears that Jesus is close to the house, she runs to meet him and she is conflicted. Her humanity cries out, "If you had been here, he wouldn't have died!" But as she looks in Jesus' eyes, her faith rallies. "I know," she adds, "that even now God will do anything you ask."

I so relate to Martha's heart. Haven't you ever been in a place where part of you wants to cry out "Why?" to God but another part believes in and longs for his will? It's the human struggle. We know that God is loving and powerful and can do anything he wants, but sometimes he doesn't do things that we believe to be in his character. Part of us wants to wail into his face, and another part of us wants to kneel at his feet.

So, too, with Martha.

Jesus assures her that Lazarus will rise again, but Martha interprets his statement as a traditional comforting belief held by the Jews that the just will live again.

Then Jesus blows the top off the whole system as he says to Martha: "You don't have to wait for the End. I am, right now, Resurrection and Life. The one who believes in me, even though he or she dies, will live. And everyone who lives believing in me does not ultimately die at all. Do you believe this?" (John 11:25–26 MSG).

Trust asks us to believe this, that Jesus brings life.

The idea sounds reasonable but it is tested in a million different ways in every life. Even Martha, running to Jesus, believing him, is thinking of her brother in the grave. You can almost see her struggle to understand: *Right, Lord. My brother will rise again—in heaven. Maybe you call us to suffer with you. Maybe things don't get better in this life. Maybe the "life" you talk about means strictly spiritual life and it begins after earthly life. Maybe you don't care so much about what happens here and now.*

No, Jesus is about to show her. Spiritual life is here; it is now.

How many times have you, like Martha, struggled, wavered in despair—or sunk into it—not seeing what you expect from God in the here and now? This is not a new struggle. Even David of the Old Testament, centuries earlier, wrestled with trust that God brings life for now, each day. He came to understand what Jesus told Martha:

I would have despaired unless I had believed that I would see the goodness of the LORD in the land of the living. Wait for the LORD; be strong and let your heart take courage; yes, wait for the LORD. (Psalm 27:13–14 NASB).

God is working on the miracle each of us needs, David is saying: He will resurrect your dreams, your purpose, your hope.

Like David, Martha rallies trust. She chooses to wait on the Lord, only she does so in her Martha way. "Yes, Lord, I believe," she tells Jesus (John 11:27), then she returns to the house to rouse her sister and tell Mary that Jesus is asking for her so get a move on.

Jesus, still on the outskirts of Bethany, waits for the sisters and exactly the right moment to glorify God in a way that will change everything. The Bible tells us, "Mary came to where Jesus was waiting and fell at his feet, saying 'Master, if only you had been here, my brother would not have died'" (v. 32 MSG). Mary, too, was heartbroken. This was her brother whom she loved, and now he was gone. The way she phrased her cry was a little different than Martha's. In the Greek the emphasis is on "my *brother*." It reads as if to say, "This wasn't just anyone who died here, Lord. It was Lazarus—my Lazarus, my brother."

This Was Never Meant to Be!

The incredulousness in Mary's cry is the shock and pain we, too, express to God when sad things happen and we experience deep loss.

Often we focus on the *why* and search for a rhyme or reason to these events, as if that would increase our trust. But rarely is the why explained. Jesus' response is:

Therefore, when Jesus saw her weeping, and the Jews who came with her weeping, He groaned in the spirit and was troubled.

And He said, "Where have you laid him?"

They said to Him, "Lord, come and see."

Jesus wept. (John 11:33–35)

From the Greek there are three words used here: *deeply moved*, *troubled*, and *wept*. The first word in Greek is *enebrimesato*, which is a very strong term that denotes fierce anger and literally translates as "to snort like a horse." I find that fascinating. I cannot believe that Christ was angry with Mary or Martha, but rather with death itself and what it does to humanity. And perhaps he is angry at the unbelief he sees around him, despite what he has already shown of the kingdom of God. It is a rare moment when we get to see how Christ feels about the fall of man and the influence of the enemy, and it explains the other two words used in this passage.

The word translated "troubled" is *etaraxen*, which denotes agitation. Jesus' humanity was deeply touched by the death of his friend and the grief of the sisters and other mourners. When we read that Jesus wept, the tense of the word is a spontaneous outburst. Jesus literally burst into tears.

"The weeping here has no connection with the surge of anger," Rudolph Schnackenburg writes, "but they are tears for the sadness and darkness of this present world."[3]

So Jesus moves toward the tomb, which would have been a chamber cut into limestone rock. Scripture repeats here that the anger Jesus has shown is still present as he faces the reality that all humanity now must embrace—death.

He tells some of the men to remove the stone from the grave's opening.

Martha is horrified. It was hard enough to bury Lazarus's

lifeless body, but to open the tomb after four days and face the stench and decomposition is too much.

Jesus senses her panic. He turns to her and reminds her to trust him. He's simple and clear here. *No matter how things appear, Martha, believe.*

So the stone is rolled from the mouth of the tomb. Jesus looks up to heaven and prays for the benefit of those listening, "Father, I'm grateful that you have listened to me. I know you always do listen, but on account of this crowd standing here I've spoken so that they might believe that you sent me" (John 11:41–42 MSG).

This prayer makes it crystal clear that Christ has already prayed for Lazarus and God has already answered. It reminds me of Psalm 118:21, in which the psalmist tells God, "I will praise You, for You have answered me." (In my book *Get Off Your Knees and Pray*, the heart of my message was that just as Christ was in constant communion with his Father, we should be too.[4])

I love what R. H. Fuller writes about this prayer of Jesus: "When he engages in vocal prayer, he is not entering, as we do, from a state of non-praying into prayer. He is only giving overt expression to what is the ground and base of his life."[5]

After thanking God for hearing his prayer, Jesus addresses his friend: "Lazarus, come out." The Greek text translates literally, "Lazarus, it's this way out," for surely Jesus is directing his friend out of a dark place.

The power of this moment cannot be lost; it's no mistake that Jesus calls Lazarus by his name. Earlier he told his disciples: "Don't act so surprised at all this. The time is coming when everyone dead and buried will hear his voice . . . [and] will walk out" (John 5:28–29 MSG). Imagine how many might have come forward if Jesus had simply said, "Come out!"

When Disappointment Turns to Dancing

I imagine there was utter silence after Jesus called on Lazarus. Then from inside the cave, you hear something. With a single sentence, in an instant, God reverses the decay of Lazarus's earthly body—his spirit reenters and restores Lazarus.

Imagine Lazarus stumbling to the edge of the cave. I'm sure the light was blinding to him at first. There he stood, a dead man walking, still dressed in his grave clothes. He has just come from a dark place and is standing on the edge of a frightening one—one calling, once again, for trust in his Savior.

Jesus, however, doesn't touch Lazarus yet. Instead, Jesus turns to Martha and Mary and instructs them to have the rags of death taken away. This is an essential point because every time we are called to trust, Jesus says, as he said to Martha at the tomb and he's said to me in my spirit many times: *No matter how things appear, believe*—believe because he is poised to do what only he can do, and he asks those who love him to do what we can do. For only Jesus can call someone from death to life, but then he asks us to do what we can do—lovingly care for that person and strip away the signs of death.

Never Before!

Now all hell truly breaks loose. By restoring Lazarus to life after four days, Jesus has not only thrown down the gauntlet to Satan and the powers of hell, but to the chief priests and Pharisees as well. Up until this point they have considered Jesus manageable, but not after this.

John recounts their response:

The high priests and Pharisees called a meeting of the Jewish ruling body. "What do we do now?" they asked. "This man keeps on doing things, creating God-signs. If we let him go on, pretty soon everyone will be believing in him and the Romans will come and remove what little power and privilege we still have." (John 11:47–48 MSG)

Indeed, bringing Lazarus back from the dead has changed everything. From this day onward, Jesus no longer walks freely in public, and in the gospels you can feel the clock begin to tick faster toward the end of his ministry on this earth.

John, in fact, is the only one of the four gospel writers who records this miracle, and he records it in great detail. Matthew, Mark, and Luke confine their narrative to Galilee, where most of Jesus' ministry occurred until the final week of his life. John gives us a rare gift, then, in recording Lazarus's amazing resurrection. Some theologians suggest that the other gospels were written before John's, and did not include the story out of respect for Lazarus's safety—because he still would have been alive at the time. Lazarus's return from the dead, after all, made him a marked man too. But by the time John's gospel was written, Lazarus would have died a second death and this time he would be safely home.

As for the onlookers that day? There were two strong reactions: those who believed and those who didn't. Many people saw the resurrection as the undeniable proof that Jesus was the Messiah. The unbelievers were angry and went to the Pharisees and chief council, who convened to hush up the event and get rid of Jesus.

Think back a moment to when Jesus stood before the tomb. Just before he calls out Lazarus, he weeps—and there are two responses from the onlookers: empathy and cynicism. The empathizers were moved by how much Jesus loved Lazarus; the cynics snarked that if Jesus loved Lazarus so much, he should have gotten there before his friend died.

How like our human nature to see either the emotion of the moment or only the what-ifs. How like the times you've pointed to something larger in a difficult circumstance, tried to share something amazing that God has done in your life, only to encounter one of these two responses.

The thing is that when Jesus brings us back to life, whether physically like Lazarus or spiritually and emotionally back from hopelessness, he evokes a response.

There will be those people who choose to stay and be part of what has taken place, as they did that day with Lazarus. They will be excited, bursting with questions like I imagine they asked Lazarus: "Where were you when you were dead; can you remember?" "What happened when you heard Jesus' voice?" "Did you see anyone you knew?" (Of course, Martha would have told them to let Lazarus go home, have a good bath and a meal, and ask their questions another day.)

But then there are others in the crowd not impressed with the miracle, which is so confusing and hurtful to those of us who believe.

A woman I'd met once told me sadly, "My husband and I are both believers but God has touched me in a fresh way recently at a retreat, and I feel so much closer to him. I thought my husband would be happy for me, but he just seems annoyed. I don't understand."

Few of us do. When God breathes life, it demands a response. Some welcome God's presence and deeply long to experience him. Others are threatened by him. Perhaps they want to hang on to their lives, believing they, not God, are in control.

I believe we will see more of this kind of duality in the coming days. It seems that as the return of Christ draws closer, the light will burn brighter and the darkness will intensify. Christ is calling to us to *Look. Look at Lazarus.* These are days to choose whom we will follow—how we will trust, no matter what the cost. Will we be like Thomas and say, *I don't know where you're going, but I want to be where you are?* Will we trust enough to take a step farther, even if it's into darkness? Do we believe that trust is not easy, but certainly life-changing?

Why the Pain?

That, of course, is the rub when it comes to trusting God. The great challenge to trust is when he allows us—or even more so, those we love—to suffer. Christians have struggled with this for two thousand years and will continue to do so until Christ returns for his church. In her deeply comforting devotional book, *Jesus Calling*, missionary Sarah Young writes this, which she believes came right from the heart of God:

> From your limited human perspective, it may look as if I'm mismanaging things. But you don't know what I know or see what I see. If I pulled back the curtain to allow you to view heavenly realms, you would understand much more. However, I have designed you to live by faith and not by sight.[6]

Mary and Martha realized this design when their lives were transformed by trusting God. They never received answers as to why they had to watch Lazarus die the first time, but they learned a few powerful truths about God's design.

First, the sisters learned they could tell Jesus the truth, even the truth about their anger and frustration, their fear and doubt and hurt. They didn't have to pretend that they were fine with

Christ's apparently tardy arrival. They voiced their pain and took it right to Jesus.

It took me a long time to learn that. Although the very idea seems ridiculous to me now, I used to want God to perceive me to have more faith and trust than I really had. If I was hurt or confused by God's silence, I stuffed those feelings deep inside and presented my "good side" to God. But unspoken pain festers and takes on a life of its own; it cripples growth. Now I trust God's love for me enough to tell him what I honestly feel knowing that just as he received Mary and Martha, he will receive me.

Another lesson I see is unspoken but must have been present. Mary and Martha both watched Jesus weep. They must have realized that Jesus knew that he was about to bring Lazarus back to life, and yet he shed tears of grief and outrage for the brokenness of the human condition.

To me, that adds a holy dignity to so many of life's harshest moments. It says we can trust in a Savior who cares—deeply. It says he has a plan and in the midst of working it takes the time to feel with us, hurt with us, hear us.

How beautiful. How stirring. How much it makes me want to be with Jesus, go a long distance with him, and trust in him.

Of course, as Mary, Martha, and Lazarus experienced, that journey of trust can plunge us into darkness until even the path disappears before our eyes. When I found myself in such a season of spiritual darkness, I discovered that there was someone sitting beside me on the road, and he had been there before.

SIX

INTO THE DARKNESS TO FIND THE LIGHT

The Beauty of Seeing

No one can bar the road to truth, and to advance its cause
I'm ready to accept even death.

—ALEXANDER SOLZHENITSYN

When he got to the outskirts of Damascus, he was suddenly
dazed by a blinding flash of light. As he fell to the ground,
he heard a voice: "Saul, Saul, why are you out to get me?" He
said, "Who are you, Master?"

—ACTS 9:3–5 MSG

I grew up predisposed to dislike the apostle Paul. I blame this on Mr. Hornal, one of the deacons in the church of my childhood. To be fair, Mr. Hornal was a good man. He appeared quite stern but had a kind heart. He did, however, fully embrace what he understood to be the apostle Paul's theology as it pertains to women in the church. So if I ever dared to wear pants to the evening service on a Sunday night, he considered that a disgrace, as I was now attired like a man. Mr. Hornal and I had quite a discussion when I cut my long hair too. He believed that my long hair was "my glory," and I had left my glory on the floor of the beauty salon in Hourston's department store.

When I sang in church, which I did fairly often, Mr. Hornal expected that it should always be an appropriate hymn from the book we used for Sunday evening services, *The Redemption Hymnal*. The first time that I sang a song by Jamie Owens, an American contemporary Christian artist, Mr. Hornal stopped me as I attempted to creep past him. He asked me in a tone ripe with disapproval, "What number was that in *The Redemption Hymnal?*"

So in my young mind, if Mr. Hornal was an ardent disciple of the apostle Paul, then Paul must have been a cranky single guy who messed with things that were not his business.

I couldn't have been more wrong—about Mr. Hornal or Paul.

Both loved God deeply. They wanted to protect his laws and, more, they wanted everyone to do the same—to follow God correctly, completely, fully. They didn't trust that God, the creator of those laws, would lead us to correct, complete, full lives in his way, his time.

So Paul's passion for being an ensurer of the faith became so strong that it clouded his vision to the point of destroying the faith he loved. Paul began to focus so much on keeping the law that he failed to see the whole spirit behind it. He couldn't see—distrust blinded him to it—how God has it all in control and just wants our trust. Paul lost his way.

How did he get so far from what he believed anyway?

Worlds Apart

No one is sure of the exact dates of the birth of Christ and Saul, who later became known as Paul, but it is likely they were born within months of each other. And though they were both raised in Jewish homes to be ready for the Christ—for Jesus to fulfill being the Christ—their worlds could not have been more different. Look at the differences, from their very beginnings on earth.

A Boy Born into Poverty

It was a cold night, so the stars stood out like perfectly placed diamonds in the sky. "It should be any minute now," the husband whispered as he watched his young wife lying on the straw, her face twisted by pain. *It shouldn't be like this. She should have her mother here*, he thought. *She should be in a warm bed with all those she loves around her, not just me. What help can I be?* With one final heart-wrenching cry, his son was thrust into this world.

"Look at him, Mary. He's beautiful."

Mary cradled the little mouth to her breast and tried to keep the baby warm. Joseph cleaned him as best he could and gave Mary a warm cloth to wrap their tiny one. At the back of the stable, a cow moved around in the straw and dust filled the air.

"I wish my mother were here, Joseph," Mary said. She shifted on the straw, trying to make herself more comfortable. She was so tired and sore, and yet as she gazed at the top of her baby's head, tiny black curls still damp on his neck, she knew that she had been born for this moment. "Do you hear that, Jesus?" she whispered. "Can you hear the music? It's so beautiful. I hear angels singing."

A Boy Born into Privilege

"It should be any moment now, my dear," the man assured his wife. "The nurse says you are doing so well. I love you and am very proud of you. I will be just outside the door if you need me."

"Do you think it will be a son?" she asked her husband, Benjamin.

"If God's favor shines on us this night, my dear, it will be a boy."

Benjamin paced up and down the marble corridor outside the bedroom.

"Jehovah, God of Abraham, Isaac, and Jacob, if you have given us a boy, this night he will be dedicated as none before to you and to your law."

Suddenly there was a cry, a strong cry from inside the chamber. In moments the nurse came out to Benjamin and placed the baby in his arms, announcing, "You have a son, sir, a beautiful, healthy baby boy!"

"We will call him Saul," his father said. "Welcome into the world, my precious son. Welcome!"

Opposites Do Attract

Jesus was born into a humble family of Jews living in Nazareth. His father, Joseph, was a carpenter, so it's likely that Jesus adopted his father's trade until it was time to begin his public ministry.

Although Joseph was not Jesus' biological father (because Jesus was conceived by the Holy Spirit), Matthew's gospel lists Joseph as his legal father, placing Christ in the line of David. We don't know much about the education he received, but even by the age of twelve he was able to sit with the teachers in the synagogue and ask probing questions about the Law and the prophets. His mother, Mary, was very devout. Having been visited by the angel Gabriel, who told her about this child she would conceive by God, I'm sure that she and Joseph taught Jesus as much as they knew about their faith.

Saul, on the other hand, was born into a family of wealth, respect, and privilege. Saul's parents lived in Tarsus, the capital city of Cilicia in southeast Asia Minor. It was a wealthy city on the banks on the river Cydnus; there were only three universities at that time (the other two in Athens and Alexandria); the one in Tarsus was the most sought after because of its excellent reputation. Saul's father, whom I fictitiously named Benjamin, came from the purest of the pure Jewish lines. He was from the tribe of Benjamin, a tribe known for its unmixed and untainted bloodline.

Paul later wrote to the church in Philippi, "You know my pedigree: a legitimate birth, circumcised on the eighth day; an Israelite from the elite tribe of Benjamin; a strict and devout adherent to God's law; a fiery defender of the purity of my religion" (Philippians 3:4–5 MSG).

As far as Jewish tribes were concerned, Paul was a Rockefeller. Not only was he of the highest standing as a Jew, but his father was a Roman citizen, which made Saul what was known as "freeborn." We are not told how his father received this unusual gift. Roman citizenship could be bought or awarded by some great service to the state, and it proved to be very useful to Saul later in life, though not in the way his father might have imagined or chosen.

It was decided that instead of becoming a merchant, which many boys of high-ranking families in seaports became, Saul would train to become a rabbi. His early education was in Tarsus, but at about thirteen years of age Saul was sent to Jerusalem to train under the great Gamaliel. Saul was a man set apart to serve God.

It's intriguing to think that Jesus and Saul could have bumped into each other as boys. Jesus, twelve, sat in the temple talking with the rabbis, perhaps some of whom took part in Saul's education. I wonder what Jesus and Saul would have thought of each other? Both had a hunger to learn, but their destinies would take them many miles apart. After his education was complete, Saul most likely returned to Tarsus and connected to the synagogue there. We hear nothing of him from then until after the crucifixion of Jesus.

Not long after Christ's death, however, Saul was back in Jerusalem, learning about a rising threat to the faith, a sect called the Nazarenes. There was one man in particular who was very troubling to Saul and to other members of the Jewish high council, and his name was Stephen.

What Have I Done?

Saul became a persecutor of the early church, believing with everything that was in him that he was serving God. When he heard that a Jew, a man called Stephen, was saying that a crucified Jewish radical was the long-awaited Messiah, Saul was furious. Stephen was eventually handed over to the religious court and put on trial. Many of the Jews who stood against Stephen did so because of petty jealousy rather than strong conviction.

The early church was growing very fast, but just as God was blessing their growth, some people thought that certain groups in the church were getting better treatment than others. The

Greek-speaking Christians thought that the Hebrew-speaking Christians were getting favored treatment when food was shared out. To try to smooth these troubled waters, the apostles, not wanting to be distracted from their call, decided that seven men would be appointed deacons to make sure that there was no favoritism. Stephen was one of the seven.

Does any of this sound familiar? Isn't it amazing how often as believers we get trapped in what doesn't matter and miss the whole point of what we believe? Many of these people had listened as Jesus taught on the hillsides of Galilee. They had seen miracles, and now they were arguing because "Your wife got a bigger loaf of bread than my wife!" So Stephen and the six other men did everything they could to restore harmony among the believers.

God used Stephen in other powerful ways too. Miracles took place when he prayed—but just as with the raising of Lazarus, when God shows up in ways where heaven invades earth, it evokes a powerful response. Some of the Jews from Asia Minor who were converted slaves did not like what was happening through Stephen, so they began to plot against him. Jealousy is a powerful thing in the hands of the enemy. It can blind us to the truth and drive us to do the unthinkable. So they paid men to lie about Stephen, saying that he had cursed God and Moses.

So Stephen was put on trial. As he stood in the dock, we read that no one in the court could take their eyes off him because his face glowed like an angel. Even though Stephen faced a brutal end through stoning, he was gifted with a clear picture of Christ, who was waiting to receive him home.

When persecution and difficulty arise, grace abounds even more. I take great comfort in that. We don't know what the next few years might look like in the world, but we have the testimony of thousands that when we are asked to give an account of the hope within us, God's grace and strength will overflow. Those who put Stephen on trial were about to witness that.

Making the Most of a Public Platform

Early in my music career, I toured seventy cities with legendary guitarist Phil Keaggy. I have never worked with a more talented musician. One night after a concert we arrived back at our hotel and were hungry. The restaurant was closed, but they told us that we could order sandwiches in the bar and take them to our rooms. So we placed an order and waited for them to be made.

A man on a corner stage was singing and playing some old classic songs on guitar in the bar, and Phil must have been talking too loudly, understandably upsetting to the artist performing. But the musician stopped in the middle of a song, pointed at Phil, and said through his microphone, "Could you do any better?"

Phil looked at the rest of us, and we said, "Go for it!"

Phil apologized to the man for interrupting his flow, took his guitar, and for the next forty-five minutes played and sang his heart out. I felt so sorry for the bar singer. He said at the end of Phil's set, "Well, I'll never do that again!" That's kind of what Stephen's accusers did too. When you give someone a platform, you cannot always control what will happen.

Stephen's accusers gave him a public platform to defend himself, and he used it—but not in the way they thought he would. They thought he would beg for his life and plead his innocence. He did not; instead, he used his moment to give an account of how stubborn the Jewish people have been through history and ended with the greatest indictment of all, their failure to recognize God's Messiah:

And you continue, so bullheaded! Calluses on your hearts, flaps on your ears! Deliberately ignoring the Holy Spirit, you're just like your ancestors. Was there ever a prophet who didn't get the same treatment? Your ancestors killed anyone who dared talk about the coming of the Just One. And you've kept up the family tradition—traitors and murderers, all of you. You had God's Law handed to you by angels—gift-wrapped!—and you squandered it! (Acts 7:51–53 MSG)

Stephen's powerful accusations made the crowd go wild with hatred, and they dragged him out of the courtroom. Luke writes in the book of Acts that Stephen was almost oblivious to the screaming mob, "But Stephen, full of the Holy Spirit, hardly noticed—he only had eyes for God, whom he saw in all his glory with Jesus standing at his side. He said, 'Oh! I see heaven wide open and the Son of Man standing at God's side!'" (Acts 7:55–56 MSG).

After hearing these words, the members of the Sanhedrin, the Jewish ruling council, dragged Stephen out of town and began to pelt him with rocks. Stoning was the accepted form of execution in the Jewish community, and Roman rule allowed for different religious groups to practice their own laws. The ringleaders took off their coats and asked a young man to watch over them while they finished executing Stephen. That man was Saul. When Stephen was dead, Saul congratulated them on doing such a good job. He had no idea that he had just watched them stone a man whom one day he would stand beside around the throne of God.

Let the Games Begin

Stephen's stoning became a catalyst for intense Jewish persecution of the church, and the man at the forefront of it all was Saul.

Scripture tells us, "Saul just went wild, devastating the church, entering house after house after house, dragging men and women off to jail" (Acts 8:3 MSG).

It's ironic to think that as Saul got up each morning and prayed that God would give him the strength to find all the followers of The Way and drag them back to prison in Jerusalem, those very ones were praying to the same God for wisdom and courage to face what lay ahead.

I find Saul's conversion a very moving story because God took Saul into a dark night to show him the light. Ever been there?

One Sunday Morning

I had been in the psychiatric hospital for three weeks. So much of my time there was very painful, digging up all the things I was afraid of and looking at them. I felt like such a failure. I had built my whole life on being useful to God and to his people, so when that collapsed, I felt little reason to live. One of the things that tormented me was what would happen to the people who had written to me over the years to say how much God had used me to help them. What would happen when they found out that I was in a psychiatric hospital? Would they throw everything away because the vessel was so flawed? I wept many bitter tears over that.

One Sunday morning, a small group of patients asked if we could go to a local church. We had been at the ward long enough to earn a pass, so the transport was arranged and two nurses went with us. We filled the back row of a small Episcopalian church on the outskirts of Washington, D.C. It was a cool but sunny fall day, and the rays of sunlight through stained-glass windows bounced off the polished pews. How peaceful, to sit there and watch other people file in; some with smiles on their faces and others seeming distracted or rushed. The hymns were old and familiar, and I liked that. I wasn't in the mood for anything new or trendy. I wanted to hear the songs I have known since I was a child.

We sang one that I have loved all my life, written by a fellow Scot, George Matheson:

> *O Love that wilt not let me go,*
> *I rest my weary soul in thee;*
> *I give thee back the life I owe,*
> *That in thine ocean depths its flow*
> *May richer, fuller be.*
>
> *O light that followest all my way,*
> *I yield my flickering torch to thee;*
> *My heart restores its borrowed ray,*
> *That in thy sunshine's blaze its day*
> *May brighter, fairer be.*
>
> *O Joy that seekest me through pain,*
> *I cannot close my heart to thee;*
> *I trace the rainbow through the rain,*
> *And feel the promise is not vain,*
> *That morn shall tearless be.*
>
> *O Cross that liftest up my head,*
> *I dare not ask to fly from thee;*
> *I lay in dust life's glory dead,*
> *And from the ground there blossoms red*
> *Life that shall endless be.*

When Matheson was asked about the circumstances sur-rounding the writing of the words, he said:

My hymn was composed in the manse of Innelan, Scotland when I was 40 years of age. I was alone in the manse at that time. Something happened to me, which was known only to myself, and which caused me the most severe mental suffering. The hymn was the fruit of that suffering. It was the quickest bit of work I ever did in my life. I am quite sure that the whole work was completed in five minutes. I have no natural gift of rhythm. All the other verses I have ever written are manufactured articles; this came like a dayspring from on high.[1]

Matheson had no way of knowing then that the fruit of his suffering would bring so much comfort through the years to others who suffered too. Nor could he have known that his words would travel across the water to America and into a small church on a certain Sunday a hundred and ten years later and lift the head of a very broken Scottish girl.

When the priest stood to deliver his sermon that Sunday, I listened intently and prayed for God to show me something beyond what I understood. I felt as if everything I had built my life upon had fallen apart, and I was desperate for help. I remember the priest saying that some of us there that morning felt as if we were buried alive and the air was becoming very thin. He said, "Jesus is here. All you have to do is reach out a hand, and he will pull you to safety. You don't have to save yourself; you never did."

It's Never Been About You

Those words, that idea, stung me. I felt as if Christ himself stood before me and turned on the light in my darkness. It made me squint. I had been a Christian for twenty-five years, and I finally understood that my salvation was not about me working hard enough to make God love me. That sounds so simple as I see the words on paper, but if you have ever been in that punishing place where nothing you do will ever be enough, you understand. My eyes began to water, as they do when struck by a blinding light, and I wept tears of pure joy.

Sometimes I have to work hard to remind myself of things I know to be true, but whatever happened to me that day really took. I have never felt from that day until this, seventeen years later, that there is anything I can do to make God love me more or love me less. I revel in that truth more than I know how to put words to.

How does that truth resonate with you? Where do you stand in regard to God's absolute, unconditional love for you? Do you feel as if God approves of you more on some days than others? If you imagine a room full of well-known Christians and you slip in at the back, do you think Christ would want to spend as much time with you as he might with, say, Billy Graham or Beth Moore?

God's love is a hard thing to fully grasp, as it will never be found anywhere else but in his heart, but there is nothing in this life that I am more convinced of. Right now, with everything you dislike about yourself and all the dark places you hide, you are absolutely loved by God.

Who Are You?

The persecution of the early believers simply turned them into missionaries as they were scattered all across the region. Saul heard that some had traveled as far as Damascus, about 130 miles from Jerusalem. He obtained letters from the chief rabbi in Jerusalem for the synagogues in Damascus and warrants for the arrest of any who claimed to be followers of The Way. With document in hand he set out on the six-day trip. Saul set out believing that God was with him on this quest to extinguish those whom he believed were blaspheming against the Lord God of Israel.

It's hard to see through the window of our twenty-first Western culture that Saul honestly thought he was on a mission from God that justified him dragging men and women from their homes to be imprisoned. There was precedence in the books of the Law for these kinds of extreme measures against blasphemers, and those are the Scriptures Saul had studied. God's command to the children of Israel in the Old Testament was to keep the faith pure and unpolluted. Saul believed that this new sect was corrupting the faith, but he had no idea that he was about to meet the author and finisher of his faith.

As he got close to Damascus, suddenly a light that burned brighter than the sun surrounded him. Saul fell off his horse and as he lay on the ground he heard a voice, "Saul, Saul, why are you persecuting Me?" (Acts 9:4). The fact that the light and the voice were coming from heaven made it clear to Saul that he was being addressed by God. Can you imagine his confusion? Saul had dedicated his life to God's work, no matter what it cost him personally—and now God was accusing him of persecuting the God he loved?

What Have I Done?

Saul's confusion was soon extended to shock and, over the next few days, I'm sure, deep grief as the Voice told him, "I am Jesus, the One you're hunting down. I want you to get up and enter the city. In the city you'll be told what to do next" (Acts 9:5–6 MSG).

When Saul stood up after his encounter with the resurrected Lord, he was completely blind.

Perhaps Christ gave him a physical picture of a spiritual truth: *Saul, you think you can see clearly, but you are blind to what is true.*

Saul's servants led him into the city. For three days, Saul didn't eat or drink as he prayed and considered the implications of what he had been told:

- Although he believed that he had given his life to serving God, he had just been rebuked from heaven. How could he have believed himself to be so right and yet have been so wrong?
- This Jesus was alive, so his death, rather than being one of a traitor, was the death of Messiah as the prophet Isaiah had foretold (Isaiah 9). How could he have missed this?
- Something new was happening here. Jesus had asked Saul, "Why are you persecuting *me*?" As far as Saul understood, he had done nothing to Jesus, only to his followers. Did Jesus' statement mean that if you wounded one of Christ's followers, you wounded him?

What Now, Lord?

Have you ever experienced a season in your life when you lost your way? Perhaps you were involved in the women's ministry in your church and through misunderstanding or misrepresentation, you found yourself out in the cold. Or you were working with a group of friends, on the job, or in your neighborhood, trying to make something happen, and suddenly your sure footing was gone; you found yourself on the floor, not even sure what happened.

Is God still in control?

I mentioned in an earlier chapter that there was a person I had counted as a friend who turned against me suddenly after I left the Christian Broadcasting Network. This person believed that because I had spent a month in a psychiatric hospital and was now on antidepressant medication, I was not to be trusted.

I was devastated when I learned this person made several calls to churches I had worked with and stores that carried my books and CDs, saying a lot of damaging things that had some truth in them but were not the whole truth.

Yet I was too exhausted and brokenhearted to even try to fight back.

Then God spoke to me through his Word:

> Listen carefully: Unless a grain of wheat is buried in the ground, dead to the world, it is never any more than a grain of wheat. But if it is buried, it sprouts and reproduces itself many times over. In the same way, anyone who holds on to life just as it is destroys that life. But if you let it go, reckless in your love, you'll have it forever, real and eternal. (John 12:24–25 MSG)

Jesus is saying: let go of whatever it is you are trying to hold onto. If you are trying to hold onto a life, a ministry, a position, or a career that doesn't please God, then let it die. Trust him, instead of yourself, to accomplish his will. If he is involved, then in his time, he will let what you let go bloom once again.

I found that when I feel lost or confused, I can navigate the worst places by resting on, trusting in, God's revealed Word. If all you see around you at the moment is darkness and confusion, don't lose heart—God might be about to resurrect your life in ways you could not imagine.

Just look at what happened to Paul.

Sistor Vera

951-
352-3301

Tell What to Whom?

The men who were traveling with Saul got him to Damascus where he stayed with Judas, a man from one of the prominent synagogues. For three days he didn't eat or drink; he just prayed. I wonder what went on in Saul's mind and heart during that dark time. Did he think his blindness was permanent? Did he wonder if he would ever hear from God again or think his intense persecution of the followers of Christ disqualified him from his love?

God answered Saul's prayers and sent a Christian named Ananias to pray for him. Ananias was understandably reluctant at first—after all, Saul was known for dragging Christians to prison. Ananias wanted to be sure that God knew what Saul had been up to (ever tried to argue with God?), but God told him to go and that he would find Saul praying. It was just as God had said. When Ananias saw Saul, this man who had been so full of fury and now seemed so full of uncertainty moved his heart. Ananias laid hands on Saul and prayed for him. His blindness was immediately lifted, and he asked to be baptized.

After his baptism, Paul spent time away from Jerusalem for a while. Paul's letter to the Galatians tells us that he spent time in Arabia, but it is not clear how long. "Immediately after my calling—without consulting anyone around me and without going up to Jerusalem to confer with those who were apostles long before I was—I got away to Arabia. Later I returned to Damascus" (Galatians 1:16–17 MSG).

We're not told what took place during that time or how long he spent alone seeking the face of Christ, but it would seem clear that he spent it studying and preparing for the mission that was ahead of him, which would be a very costly one. I can only imagine what it must have been like for someone as devout as Saul to come to terms with what he had been part of. He must have thought back to Stephen and others who had suffered and even died for the faith he now embraced.

A New Beginning

Saul (who would later become known by his Roman name, Paul, as his call extended to the Gentile world) became as fervent a proclaimer of the truth of Jesus Christ crucified and resurrected as he had once fervently opposed those who believed. For the rest of Paul's life he served the risen Christ and remained true to his unique calling to take the gospel to the non-Jewish world. Ten years after his conversion, he began planting churches in Asia Minor and Europe. His letters to those churches, although great theological works, were real letters sent to real men and women who were struggling with their faith. For one who was such a student of the law, his message was soaked in grace.

Forgiven Much and Loving Much

Rather than the cranky apostle I once foolishly dubbed him, Paul was a tender man who loved and nurtured believers. Perhaps his dark night tenderized his heart.

Think of the people who have helped you most through their writing, their friendship, or their leadership, and you'll notice something they have in common: broken vessels seem to be uniquely crafted to carry grace. Paul never compromised the gospel of Christ, but he brought it with a tender heart and compelling passion so that others would know this Jesus who had saved him.

One of the other things of note is that Paul became a team

player. No longer a man on a fiery solo mission, the apostle Paul treasured his friends and coworkers in the gospel. Paul drew others into the work. He became a mentor for young church leaders like Timothy, whom he referred to as a beloved son. Compassion and community seem to be the hallmarks of those who have been brought though a dark night to a new day.

The Marks of Grace

Paul went on to suffer greatly for his faith. Five times he received the maximum Jewish punishment of thirty-nine lashes with a whip. Three times he was beaten with rods and he was stoned almost to death. He was in three shipwrecks, one that left him in the sea all day and night. By the end of his life, Paul's sight was failing him and he spent his days shackled to a Roman guard. If you were to peer into his jail cell I doubt that he would seem to be a great leader who would be used by God to shape the church.

When Paul's first, two-year-long imprisonment came to an end, it was a short-lived liberty. That year after several days of rioting, Rome burned and the evil emperor Nero (whom history credits with starting the fire) blamed it on the Christians. Paul was rearrested and dragged back to Rome to appear before this tyrant. What a strange picture that makes for me: a small-minded, debauched emperor sitting draped in purple robes passing judgment on this humble servant of God.

The trial ended, and Paul was condemned to death. Though his execution isn't described in Scripture, I am sure that as he knelt beside the block and the executioner raised his sword, Christ stood ready to welcome this faithful servant home.

Trust had to have changed Paul almost more than anyone I know. He started out so sure of who he was, so certain of his place as one chosen by God, the purest of the pure. Then in a flash, one moment, everything he had built his life on was pulled out from underneath him—he had to start all over again.

Here is where I find Paul's trust in the absolute love and grace of God so helpful—he had to base it on the same things that you and I do.

For years he had based his assurance on keeping the rules. As a proud Jew, he could put his head on the pillow at night mentally ticking off every rule that he had upheld, but not anymore. Now he had to put his trust in the finished work of Christ, which is something we all struggle with. There is something in us that wants to feel we bring something to the table when we come to faith but we don't. We come by faith, accepting what Christ has done for us. When we finally are able to grasp hold of that truth, it is the most liberated we will ever be. As he wrote to the Church in Galatia,

> Can't you see the central issue in all this? It is not what you and I do—submit to circumcision, reject circumcision. It is what *God* is doing, and he is creating something totally new, a free life! (Galatians 6:15 MSG)

I look forward to the day when I will be able to see Paul with my own eyes and thank him for the legacy he left for you and me. Through Paul, I understand that no matter how wrong you have been, it is never too late to change—and when you do, you will love as you never knew you could. A man like Paul would only understand from heaven's perspective how God has used his life.

I wonder if you are like that and you don't even know it. Some of us have careers or callings that are more public than others. Others faithfully live their lives, day after day, doing jobs that are taken for granted or largely overlooked—for instance, those who are housebound but who pray and consider it a holy honor, or those who serve the poor and the homeless, expecting nothing in return.

There are thousands of men and women who will have no idea of the impact of their lives until they stand before Christ. But a woman named Tabitha was given the unusual privilege of coming back to life and seeing with her own eyes the legacy she had left behind.

SEVEN

THE LIFE OF CHRIST IN US

The Beauty of a Quiet Trust

Do all the good you can, to all the people you can, in all the
ways you can, as often as ever you can, as long as you can.

—CHARLES HADDON SPURGEON

Now there was in Joppa a disciple named Tabitha. . . . She was
full of good works and acts of charity. In those days she became
ill and died, and when they had washed her, they laid her in an
upper room. . . . All the widows stood . . . weeping and
showing tunics and other garments that [Tabitha] made while
she was with them. But Peter put them all outside, and knelt
down and prayed; and turning to the body he said, "Tabitha,
arise." And she opened her eyes, and when she saw Peter she
sat up. And he gave her his hand and raised her up. Then
calling the saints and widows, he presented her alive.

—ACTS 9:36–37, 39–41 ESV

I learned very quickly in my marriage that Barry likes to get the mail. Now, when I say *likes*, I am being extremely conservative. He would knock me over if he thought I might get to the mailbox first! I've never quite understood his passion. It's not as if he's waiting to hear if he has been accepted into the space program or made it onto *American Idol*. He just loves to get the mail, so I steer clear of our little black box.

When Barry brings in the day's mail, he has a routine. He separates bills from catalogs from the other junk mail, and if there is anything personal for me, he puts it on my desk. I don't get very much personal mail these days. Most of my friends communicate with me by phone, e-mail, through text-messages, or online tools. But my mom still writes letters, and I love receiving an envelope with her familiar handwriting on the address.

One day a few weeks ago, I saw what appeared to be a personal letter on my desk with a typewritten envelope. I didn't recognize the sender, but I opened the envelope and read the note addressed to me. It was from a family service counselor at a local funeral home; she declared her main passion in life to be helping people get ready for their impending demise. She had included a glossy, full-color brochure of available burial sites, which ranged in price from $179,000 to $1,725,000.

I realize that such matters are not comical, but I couldn't help laughing at some of the big marketing features. Among the offerings:

- "Select sites for couples on the lake." *A trifle soggy, I would have thought.*
- "Select sites for families at the roadside." *For drive-by visitation?*

· "A hedged property that accommodates one to eight people depending on design and family desires." *Or how large each family member is?*

The counselor signed off by saying that she would be happy to answer any questions.

I had only one: "What do you know that I don't?" *I mean, I know I've been looking a little pale recently, but this seems a bit extreme.*

The Business of Death

The whole business of death is strange to me. I find it hard to wrap my head around the fact that one moment, a person is alive, fully aware, and present; the next moment, that person can be simply gone.

The moment before my father-in-law, William, passed away, we had been talking. Then he wasn't breathing, and then . . . nothing, emptiness, his body was simply a shell. I have never experienced a more radical awareness of what it means for the spirit to be absent from the body. It was clear to me that William was not present. I knew he was with the Lord.

We had the funeral service in Charleston, South Carolina, where William had lived all his life, and it was touching to see the crowd of people who came to pay their last respects. Family members were there, church friends, and men who had worked with William years before. Everyone I talked with shared the same thing: William was great fun and loved to laugh.

What a simple, sweet legacy, and certainly how I will always remember William.

A Life in Eight Verses

Some of the most influential people are quiet, never standing on a stage or in a spotlight, never directing companies of thousands or managing caches of millions. By that same token, some of the greatest legacies are simple—not the great empire built or outstanding record set, but the laughter given, passion spent, and complete love and trust left.

We don't have great annals about a woman named Tabitha in the New Testament. Her whole story is told in eight verses in chapter nine of Acts, wedged between the accounts of two of the New Testament's most famous men: Saul's conversion to Paul, and details of Peter's ministry.

But if you look closely at those verses you'll see a woman's influential life and a great legacy marked by service to God and love and trust in him. You'll read how her death impacted everyone who knew her, and many people she'd never met.

Tabitha affects me because she shows how a quiet, simple life of trust lives on, even after your spirit leaves your body and returns to the Lord. Her service is left to every new generation like an intimate love letter to the world.

We don't know Tabitha's last name, but we know she was called Dorcas by the Greeks (Tabitha was her Hebrew name), and lived in Joppa or modern-day Jaffa.

Today the Mediterranean port city of Jaffa is considered one of the oldest cities in the world, supposed by scholars to have been established by one of Noah's sons (Japheth) after the Great Flood. In Tabitha's time, Joppa was an important city and seaport, the major port along the Mediterranean coast and for Jerusalem, which lay just thirty-five miles to the southwest.

Joppa had seen a lot of biblical history. It was the port through which Solomon brought cedar trees from Lebanon to build the temple. It was also where the prophet Jonah decided he would rather hop on a boat to Spain than visit Nineveh. I find that interesting—that it was in Joppa that Jonah ran from taking the good news to the Gentile nation of Nineveh, yet it is in Joppa that Peter receives his call to reach out to the Gentiles. So Tabitha's city is a reminder to me of how those of us who love God can be very stubborn at times, but that never thwarts the plan and purposes of God.

We also know that Tabitha is very kind, always doing good and helping the poor; and she is called a "disciple." The Hebrew word used in Acts 9:36 is *mathedria*; this is the only instance in the New Testament that the female form of "disciple" is used. I wonder if that is because Tabitha has so caught the heart of Christ in how she's lived, caring for and ministering to the poor.

Tabitha's main concern in Joppa, you see, is for destitute widows. There are plenty in this large port where husbands, fathers, and sons have launched off to sea, never to return, lost rough weather. Since there is no help from the government, widows and orphans are completely at the mercy of their community, and Tabitha does the thing she knows she can do to help. She makes clothes for them.

There is such a quiet dignity in this. Tabitha loves those who have so little. But instead of fretting about how they will be cared for, she trusts what Jesus has said, that his eye is on all the little sparrows (Matthew 6:25–34). She knows he is in control so she is free to do just what she can to give what she has in his name—and in a practical way.

I was the recipient of the grace of a Tabitha when I was a child. When my mother was widowed, she had three children under the age of seven. Many people in our church reached out to us, but one woman in particular always made sure that we were taken care of in very practical ways. She provided clothes for my sister, brother, and me; I think of her as my Tabitha.

I can only imagine what a gift Margaret Rankin was, and still is, to my mom. Her care for us was never obvious or attention seeking, never to earn respect or adoration. She would just pop over for a cup of coffee and quietly leave behind a package—and it was always just what we needed.

Not This One, Lord!

The Tabithas of this world often do their work out of the sight of others. They don't draw attention, but the impact they make is enormous, their touch on lives profound. They bring such stability and hope to others that no one can bear to lose them. God uses them in such amazing ways that if they even get sick, we respond, "Not this one, Lord!"

Such was the case when David Watson became ill. David was an Anglican priest, evangelist, author, and one of the most remarkable men I have ever met and had the joy of working alongside. When he became Curate-In-Charge of St. Cuthbert's Church, in York, England, he inherited a congregation that was all but dead. There were never more than twelve people who attended on any given Sunday. I can't imagine what it must have been like to work so hard preparing messages for such a pitiful crowd in a cold, stone sanctuary.

But David didn't see it like that. His fire for the Lord and his people consumed him—and his zeal and love showed. Word of his teaching began to spread. Soon St. Cuthbert's had outgrown its building, and the congregation moved to St. Michael-Le-Belfry, where hundreds of people began to attend every week.

David was a gentle man with a huge vision of what God's heart of love looks like. He was used all over the world and had a particular passion to see reconciliation come to Ireland, a country torn apart in the name of religion. There was a gentle grace and kindness about David that touched all who worked with him. He had written many best-selling books in England, but nothing could have prepared him for the next one he was about to begin.

Though I Walk Through the Valley

His next chapter began with a simple check-up with his doctor concerning his asthma. The visit seemed routine and as he was about to leave he mentioned needing to use the bathroom a lot lately. Was this some sign of a larger problem?

That simple, casual question set David on a path that took a radical turn downhill.

Have you ever been there? You wake up and it seems to be a day like any other, but by the time you get in bed again that night everything in your life has changed. You would give anything to turn back the clock a few hours, back to when the greatest concern was what to make for dinner that night.

That's how it was for David. He describes in his book *Fear No Evil* how he responded to the news that he had cancer:

> I was stunned. My worst fears were confirmed. I felt my throat getting dry with tension. Feebly I told him how difficult an operation was at that time, with over sixty lectures to give in California in only a few days, and with many pastors coming having already spent hundreds of dollars on this course.[1]

The specialist stressed how important it would be to have the surgery and had already booked a bed for David in Guy's Hospital. On the morning of the surgery, David read one of his favorite psalms:

You, Lord, are all I have,
And you give me all I need;
My future is in your hands. . . .
I am always aware of the Lord's presence;
He is near, and nothing can shake me.
And so I am thankful and glad,
And I feel completely secure,
Because you protect me from the power of death . . .
And the one you love you will not
Abandon to the world of the dead.
You will show me the path that leads to life;
Your presence fills me with joy
And brings me pleasure forever. (Psalm 16:5, 8–11 GNT)

When word got out that David Watson had cancer, prayer chains were set up across the United Kingdom and all around the world. Then, the morning after his surgery, David was told that the cancer had spread from his colon to his liver and was inoperable.

The specialist gave him about one year to live.

John Wimber, a longtime friend and pastor of the Anaheim Vineyard Church, heard that David was in the hospital. He and two other pastors flew from Los Angeles to London to pray for David's healing. Even though their flight was long, the three ministers went straight from Heathrow airport to David's bedside.

David described the experience: "I felt a tremendous surge of heat as well as vibrations in my body, and I knew that God was at work."

Knowing David a little, there is something touching and almost a little comical about the kinds of people his life brought together. He was a soft-spoken, tidy, disciplined, humble Anglican vicar, and yet his passion for Christ brought all sorts of other kinds of people to his side—people from every country and denominational affiliation.

In such a gathering of love and petition to God, David was convinced that Christ had healed him.

We all were. I remember discussing his situation with my mom, and our firm conviction was that God was using David in such amazing ways. God wouldn't take him home for a long time.

But we all were wrong. On the morning of February 18, 1984, David died, just thirteen months after his diagnosis. For the publication of his book *Fear No Evil*, written during the eleven months after his diagnosis, J. I. Packer was asked to write the foreword. It is one of the most moving and impactful I have ever read:

> Could it be that his dying testament will minister more widely, helping more needy people, and at a deeper level than anything he wrote before? Could it be that God accomplished more for his kingdom by taking David home as he did than he would have done by any alternate pattern of events in David's life? Most certainly it could. I know of no other book better fitted to impact to twentieth-century Christians in the West the lost wisdom about death than this one.[2]

David was just fifty years old. Thousands poured into his two memorial services in York and London, England. All who knew and loved him were impacted by his deep conviction that God was going to heal him, and yet the palpable peace he had when it became clear he was not. Even people who never knew David have been touched by his life as his books continue to speak of his love for and trust in Christ. The last words David wrote in his book were these: "Father, not my will but yours be done. In that position of security I have experienced once again his perfect love, a love that casts out all fear."

Like David, Tabitha was loved by many people who were not prepared or willing to say good-bye to her. They knew that God was alive and working on behalf of his people, and they wanted Tabitha back. They bathed her body and laid it out upstairs, but they did not anoint it for burial, as would have been the custom.

Instead, they sent for Peter:

> In those days she became ill and died, and when they had washed her, they laid her in an upper room. Since Lydda was near Joppa, the disciples, hearing that Peter was there, sent two men to him, urging him, "Please come to us without delay." (Acts 9:37–38 ESV)

New Terrain

Now Peter is in Lydda, only twelve miles from Joppa, when he gets the news about Tabitha. This is the only time Lydda (today called Lod and located just south of Israel's international airport) is mentioned in the Bible, and Peter has just experienced quite an amazing week there. He's met with a group of believers, including a man named Aeneas who has been paralyzed for eight years. Until he meets Peter, Aeneas seems to have no hope.

Upon their meeting, Peter immediately says to Aeneas, "Jesus Christ heals you. Get up and take care of your mat" (Acts 9:34 NIV); and word spreads that Peter has healed a believer in Lydda!

Remember that word of Peter's growing faith already has been spreading through the book of Acts. We read how he's been answering questions about his three years with Jesus and what it was like to see the Lord face-to-face after the resurrection. And in chapter 3, we see how Peter has met a man lame from birth, and when the man asks for money, Peter tells him that he doesn't have any money but he does have faith in the risen Christ—so get up and walk. The man does, and people begin buzzing about Peter's first recorded miracle.

So when Tabitha dies, her friends send two men to find Peter and bring him back to Joppa. I find this remarkable. No one has been raised from the dead since the death of Christ, but the Holy Spirit is moving in the lives of the young church and people are beginning to see again that with God, anything is possible.

So as Peter makes his way to Joppa, those who have been caring for Tabitha do what tradition demanded. They wash her body with warm water.

This isn't just an act of preparation for burial, but an act of desperation for hope. It was believed in those times that if there were any recoverable life in a person on death's bed, then warm water would revive the body. Imagine all the widows and ones Tabitha has helped over the years, taking turns running warm water over her brow, along her arms. Though the dead were considered unclean, the widows may not have wanted to believe their friend was deceased; maybe they took her hands in theirs, running warm cloths along the fingers gnarled with time, by work, studying the callouses and knots from all those years of sewing, serving, loving.

But Tabitha is no longer here. The hands that never rested are finally still. Her body is now just a vacant shell, and it does not take the widows long to see that their benefactor and friend, the creator of so many beautiful garments, perhaps the ones they are wearing, is . . . gone.

Heartbroken, they wrap her body in grave clothes and lay her in an upstairs room. The great scholar Dr. Lightfoot believes this is a public meeting room where believers would gather.

When Peter arrives, he is taken there and greeted by the

grieving widows. You can imagine the scene: somber, tear-filled. *Look*, they tell Peter. *See all these beautiful things Tabitha made us. Do you see how good she was to us?*

Peter sees. The room is filled with the display of Tabitha's life work, not the robes of the rich in expensive fabrics, but a tunic here and here and there, and the one this widow wears, and the others that she holds—armfuls of clothes, a room full of dresses.

He asks everyone to leave. When they are gone, he kneels beside Tabitha's body. He is modeling what he has seen Jesus do. Remember? Remember when Jesus brought Jairus's twelve-year-old daughter back to life?

> But he put them all outside and took the child's father and mother and those who were with him and went in where the child was. Taking her by the hand he said to her, "Talitha cumi," which means, "Little girl, I say to you, arise." And immediately the girl got up and began walking. (Mark 5:40–42 ESV)

On that occasion, Jesus wanted Jairus and his wife to witness what was about to happen. He allowed only Peter, James, and John to accompany him to an upper room where the lifeless body lay of a little girl. He took her hand—and that in and of itself would be shocking, as dead bodies were considered ceremonially unclean. Peter watched as the girl sat up and began to walk.

Now he is being asked to do something he has never done before: to allow the resurrection life of Christ to flow through him to this beloved woman.

We don't know what took place between Peter and Christ. All we know is that after Peter prays, he commands Tabitha to rise. He doesn't touch her until life is restored and the body is no longer a lifeless shell but breathing, full of the breath of God. Then

Peter takes Tabitha's hand, and he, too, must feel the callouses and knots there of all her love and service and trust in Christ.

The news is too amazing and cannot be contained. The story of Tabitha's resurrection spreads all over Joppa and many people give their lives to Christ.

Tabitha, we can only imagine, is not only full of joy but maybe in shock too. She has died, she has been with Jesus, and now she is back. Jesus is still with her, but everything seems so different. Her quiet life as a seamstress from Joppa is over. The one who isn't even known by more than her first name is being celebrated. She is getting news, maybe personal letters, about people she's never met who now know the Jesus she serves. She's overwhelmed and overjoyed. For now, with the church growing, she has so many new believers to help. They are poor, having given up everything to follow Christ. They trust the church will cover for them. Tabitha must have begun to think how she can put her hands and heart to work once again. For if there is one thing she knows it's how to make a mean tunic—and how to live the heart of Christ. She must have been hearing his words in her mind as she takes up her tasks anew:

> I was hungry and you fed me,
> I was thirsty and you gave me a drink,
> I was homeless and you gave me a room,
> I was shivering and you gave me clothes,
> I was sick and you stopped to visit,
> I was in prison and you came to me. (Matthew 25:35–36 MSG)

Evidence of the Life of Christ in Us

Everything Tabitha did was an offering of worship. Her gifts didn't have as much curb appeal as maybe others' gifts did. Hers were not the glamorous gifts. But she loved them and understood how God gives talents and passions and callings because he has a plan and infinite power and all he needs is the willing, trusting heart.

However, this is not an easy idea.

I spent some time with a woman who wanted to know how she could work full-time doing what I was doing: writing, traveling, and speaking.

I asked her what she was doing at the moment.

Right now, she said, she was raising six children under the age of twelve.

I was blown away and told her that I was pretty sure that what she was doing now was more than a full-time job.

Then she said something that really saddened me: "But I want to do something for God."

Where did we get the idea that the ones onstage or in bookstores are somehow more special to God? Certainly you cannot support those ideas from God's Word. I wonder if these notions come from some confusion of our Christian life with our culture's idea of success.

If we look at the full passage in Matthew, where Jesus talks about final judgment, there are some interesting elements. For the Tabithas of this world, the question will be, "Lord, when did we do the things for you that you say we did?" For those rejected at the final judgment, the antithetical question will be, "Lord, when did we ever see you in any of these predicaments and refuse to help?"

> Then those "sheep" are going to say, "Master, what are you talking about? When did we ever see you hungry and feed you, thirsty and give you a drink? And when did we ever see you sick or in prison and come to you?" Then the King will say, "I'm telling the solemn truth: Whenever you did one of these

things to someone overlooked or ignored, that was me—you did it to me." Then he will turn to the "goats," the ones on his left, and say, "Get out, worthless goats! You're good for nothing but the fires of hell. And why? Because—

I was hungry and you gave me no meal,

I was thirsty and you gave me no drink,

I was homeless and you gave me no bed,

I was shivering and you gave me no clothes,

Sick and in prison, and you never visited."

Then those "goats" are going to say, "Master, what are you talking about? When did we ever see you hungry or thirsty or homeless or shivering or sick or in prison and didn't help?"

He will answer them, "I'm telling the solemn truth: Whenever you failed to do one of these things to someone who was being overlooked or ignored, that was me—you failed to do it to me."

Then those "goats" will be herded to their eternal doom, but the "sheep" to their eternal reward. (Matthew 25:37–46 MSG)

You might reasonably question if I'm saying that good works get you into heaven. No, of course not; that would be to misunderstand what Jesus says here. Only those who have put their trust in him and in his shed blood will live with him eternally. But the heart of this passage is powerful, and I find it deeply challenging.

When we have had an encounter with the risen Christ, and he transforms our lives, he changes our hearts too. We *want* to serve, love, and show mercy—these things are evidence of a maturing faith, especially when the things that move the Son of God move our hearts too. How might our homes, our schools, and our communities be changed if every believer so pursued the heart of God that it radically impacted our behavior?

Every person is given a different gift and calling, but there is one calling that we corporately share as believers: to love without limit because that is how we are loved by God. This passage seems to indicate that it's not possible to be in relationship with Christ and remain unchanged. Not every believer has the opportunity to work with the homeless or to become involved in prison ministry, but there are many ways of being in prison.

Think of those we encounter regularly who are stuck in an internal prison of despair or hopelessness. Think of those who are homeless in terms of feeling lonely and out of place. Think of those who hunger to know more about Christ or thirst for the truth. Each of us has a call on our lives as sons and daughters of the King of kings to live aware of those around us; until we join Jesus in heaven, we love and love and love wherever God has placed us.

Love Never Dies

One of David Watson's greatest gifts to the church was the transparency of his journey. He knew without a shadow of a doubt that God was going to heal him. When John Wimber and the other pastors prayed for him, he felt God's power go through his body. He sat, many days in pain, and wrote about his faith in God.

A few weeks before his death, his writing changed a little in tone. This is one of the last paragraphs he wrote:

He showed me that all my preaching, writing and other ministry was absolutely nothing compared to my love relationship with him. God also showed me that any love for him meant nothing unless I was truly able to love from my heart my brother and my sister in Christ.[3]

I wonder what I will discover, as David did, that I knew without a shadow of a doubt to be true only to find out that in the end all I can stake my life on is the love and mercy of God. The more in love we are with our Father, the clearer we see that reaching out with his love, even when it makes us uncomfortable or we're unsure about what we're to do and what God will do, is the only way to live.

A New Day

Trust changed Tabitha. She already lived in trust when God took her—and she covered a whole community with her trust. After Peter brought her back to life, she must have been more convinced and trusting that nothing done in Christ's name is ever wasted. She also must have been unwaveringly assured that unseen acts of kindness and mercy, offered for no approval other than our heavenly Father's, are treasured by him.

For David Watson, trusting God ultimately meant putting down what he so believed to be true in order to welcome a different gift. David originally believed that God had healed him; he trusted that with his body, mind, and spirit until it became painfully clear that God was up to something else.

David's writing and his passionate preaching have always moved me, but I have never been more touched than by the final paragraphs he wrote. There is a quiet beauty and trust in his ultimate understanding that all God ever wants is the heart—your heart, my heart.

Tabitha was comfortable with her call to help the poor—it

embodied who she was, a servant to all who needed her. But what do you do when God calls you to do something that terrifies you?

I will never forget the very first Women of Faith conference where I spoke in the spring of 1997. Christian was just six weeks old, and I was still walking with a limp from a muscle that had been accidentally cut during delivery. I looked out at the crowd of women and thought I had made a terrible mistake. Barbara Johnson was going to speak about the death of two of her sons and how God had walked her through that pain. Patsy Clairmont would tell her story of years trapped in the house, imprisoned by agoraphobia. These were situations in the past that God had already delivered them from, but I was still battling depression, still on medication. I locked myself in a restroom backstage and threw up. I had shared my story once at the women's luncheon in Palm Springs but this felt so different.

For a moment I felt like I was ten years old again, and as I was getting smaller and smaller, the swing getting higher and higher. That was where I found my next friend waiting for me—and he was pretty small too.

EIGHT

TRUSTING GOD WITH YOUR FEAR

The Beauty of Taking a Step Forward

Let us be like a bird for a moment perched
On a frail branch when he sings;
Though he feels it bend, yet he sings his song,
Knowing that he has wings.

—VICTOR HUGO

One day the angel of GOD came and sat down under the oak in
Ophrah that belonged to Joash the Abiezrite, whose son Gideon
was threshing wheat in the winepress, out of sight of the
Midianites. The angel of GOD appeared to him and said, "GOD is
with you, O mighty warrior!" Gideon replied, "With *me*, my
master? If GOD is with us, why has all this happened to us?"

—JUDGES 6:11–13 MSG

When the phone rang that morning, all I could think about was how long it was going to take my pregnant self to get across the kitchen and answer it. I was forty years old, and Barry and I were expecting a child in December, just three months away. I was delighted to hear the voice of Steve Arterburn, a friend of many years. He asked me how I was doing and I told him that things were fine and we were excited about the baby.

Then Steve asked me what I considered to be a ridiculous question. He began by telling me that he had founded an organization for women called Women of Faith. There were four speakers, and ten events in churches were booked for the current year, 1996. "This thing is really exploding," he said. "We have fifteen events booked in arenas for 1997, and I wondered: Would you like to join the team?"

I was incredulous. "Steve, are you nuts? I can hardly make it across the kitchen, never mind an airport."

Never one to be deterred by an unfavorable response, Steve asked me to talk to Barry and pray about it.

I told him that I would but I saw three major problems:

1. I would be forty years old with a brand-new baby.
2. My only speaking experience so far was my trip to Palm Springs. I had never even been to a women's conference before!
3. I was still on medication for depression and didn't see myself as a candidate for an all-girls happy tour.

The strange thing was that every time I prayed about it, I felt a genuine excitement and anticipation—a side effect, I decided, of my hormones and the horse-pill prenatal vitamins I was taking. Still, the excitement wouldn't go away. Barry felt it too. Even though this seemed the least likely time to start something new, Barry also sensed that God was in this.

I called Steve and asked if I could meet any of the ladies already on the team.

The Dream Team

We met at Steve's office in Laguna Beach, California. Barbara Johnson joined us by speakerphone, and Luci Swindoll and Marilyn Meberg were there in person. I was immediately struck by how funny Marilyn was as we arm-wrestled for the only remaining Earl Grey tea bag. Luci was charming and kind, as was Barbara. Straightaway I liked these women, but that didn't change the fact that I didn't feel qualified to be a speaker.

They told me a little about themselves. Marilyn has two master's degrees, one in English and one in counseling. She had recently lost her husband, Ken, to pancreatic cancer. Luci had never married; she had been an executive with Mobil Oil for several years and had traveled all over the world. Barbara had lost two sons, one in Vietnam and one in a car wreck. She had a ministry to parents whose sons or daughters were in the homosexual lifestyle. It was called Spatula Ministries, to help parents scrape themselves off the ceiling after they recovered from the shock.

All I could see was how eminently qualified these women were to reach out to other women—and how little I could offer. Surely I would sink as they sailed through the speaker demands. Even if I could come up with a talk, would I be able to remember it? Severe clinical depression can affect the memory, so I wasn't sure.

Then these women interrupted my thinking. "Tell us a bit about yourself," they said.

Come Out, Come Out Wherever You Are

If you have been to a Women of Faith conference during the last thirteen years, you may think that I feel perfectly at ease onstage. That was not always so, and certainly not that morning in Steve's office. As I looked into Marilyn's, Luci's, and Steve's eyes that morning, I remember thinking, *Oh well, at least I got the Earl Grey tea bag.*

I told them a little about my father's death and how that had affected my life. Then I told them about what I saw as my great weakness: my battle with depression. "It's not as if I'd had a brain tumor and they took it out and now I was fine—I'm fixed," I said. "As far as I know, I might not be 'fixed' for quite some time, if ever."

I don't know how I expected them to react, but I was stunned by what they did. They hugged me. That seemingly small act was huge, like a hand reaching into my ocean of doubt and fear. I'd seen my story as alienating, something to separate me from others who were strong and put-together. Without words and with an ordinary gesture, they bridged that gap.

I thanked them for their kindness but still floundered with the idea of joining them. I had a huge problem, I said. "I don't have any talks."

"What do you mean?" Steve asked.

"Well, you know, talks like: 'Ten lessons we can learn from the life of Ruth' or 'Are your oil lamps full or do you need a top-off?' or 'A sheep's perspective of the Twenty-Third Psalm.'"

Luci laughed. "We don't do a lot on the life of farm animals!"

"But you know what I mean," I said. "I'm not a Bible study leader or a conference speaker. I could dry up halfway through 'hello.' You all know how to do this, but I don't."

"You can do it," Marilyn said. "Just tell your story."

Just Take the Next Step

I drove down to the beach after our meeting and walked along the edge of the water, praying and sensing God's response to my questions.

"I don't think I can do this, Lord."

I know.

"I don't think I want to; it terrifies me."

I know.

"At the moment, only a few people know that I spent a month in a psych ward. But if I do this, thousands and thousands of people will know." I looked out on the ocean. In the distance the waters were so deep.

Just take the next step and follow me.

Have you ever been there, on the edge of something—something familiar on one side, and on the other is the deep, dark unknown? Have you ever felt God calling you to a place you didn't want to go? Perhaps you've been asked to do something and you feel as if you are the least qualified to do the job? The fear you experience, even the thought of it, can be paralyzing.

For many years I struggled with the discrepancy between what I believed to be God's call on my life and my perceived inability to do it. Take my singing career, for example. I knew God had given me a good voice and I could sing, but I got so nervous onstage that it interfered with my performance. My voice would shake and I would struggle to breathe. It was so frustrating because I could sing perfectly well in my hotel room, but drag me to the venue, turn off the house lights, stick a microphone in my hand, put me onstage, and everything changed.

What do you do with fear when God calls you to take a next step? Do you wait for him to take away the fear before you move or do you wade through the fear and see what God will do? Where do you find the strength to push beyond that edge, to take that first step? Is courage a gift or does it have its own learning curve?

An Israelite named Gideon wrestled with all these questions.

Most people remember Gideon as a young man of Old Testament times—living in that difficult period of Israel's history between the death of the patriarch Joshua and the rise of King David. This was a time when even though the Israelites had pledged their loyalty to God, swearing to put their trust in him, they quickly abandoned much of what they believed and tried to take matters into their own hands.

And they did so badly.

In their midst is Gideon, who, facing many of his own choices, hears God. Only is it God? Gideon asks God for a sign, and about which way to go. He wants to trust God, but he's not sure how. Gideon's story, then, tells us about how to trust when you're on the edge of something, when you're uncertain and looking for direction, and when you're afraid to go forward but know you can't go back.

Trusting God in the Unknown

When we first meet Gideon in Judges 6, he is threshing wheat in a winepress. Now a winepress is a pit carved deep into rock. Threshing floors, on the other hand, are typically about thirty feet in diameter, smooth and flat, and located in exposed areas—where wind can blow away the straw and leave behind the grain after threshing.

For threshing, the wheat is cut down by sickles and either stored or scattered right across the threshing floor. A large stone would be fixed to a horse or an ox that's led around in circles, treading over the wheat, pounding out the heavy beads of grain, separating it from the chaff. This process would take about a month, even with the help of a beast of burden and a large thresh-ing floor; and then the thresher would pray for a good, strong wind to blow away the chaff and straw.

So when you see Gideon in a narrow pit in the ground, beat-ing small amounts of wheat at a time, by hand, it becomes clear that he is carefully trying to save every bit of grain possible. He's taking no chances on the wind blowing away even a small handful.

His people, after all, are desperate to salvage anything they can to eat.

Hard Years

For seven years, the Israelites' lives were miserable. God was so angry at their continuous rebellion that he allowed their enemies, the Midianites, to devastate their camps. The Midianites were desert people, camel riders, who would race in at harvest and steal or destroy Israel's crops and take the animals and any spoils. The people of Israel literally had to take to the hills just to survive, and their losses were crippling, their land left desolate. The people were starving.

Imagine losing your crop season after season: barley, wheat, grapes, olives—all the staples of your life are gone. After seven years of this, the people, Gideon's people, are also desperate.

I find it interesting that it took seven years for them to be desperate enough to ask God for mercy.

When the people finally see that their ways aren't working, they cry out to God, and he sends a prophet, whose name we don't know, to tell how all these disasters are because of their continual rebellion against him:

GOD, the God of Israel, says, I delivered you from Egypt, I freed you from a life of slavery; I rescued you from Egypt's brutality and then from every oppressor; I pushed them out of your way and gave you their land. And I said to you, "I am GOD, your God. Don't for a minute be afraid of the gods of the Amorites in whose land you are living." But you didn't listen to me. (Judges 6:7–10 MSG)

It's easy to pass judgment on the Israelites. They have seen God's deliverance in so many powerful ways, miracle after miracle, and still have not offered him wholehearted trust and devotion.

Are we so different? I have seen God do amazing things for my family, and I've sunk into such depths where I felt no hope at all and then God lifted me through the despair. I've been hit by a new challenge, then slipped back into trying to float on my own or fix things myself or, sadly, allow myself to drown in my anxiety.

This happens more than I or any of us would like to admit, this ebb and flow of trust. Just as I was studying about Gideon, in fact, I received news that a project I'd been working on for next year was being cancelled due to the bad economy. This was quite a major project and I suddenly felt that familiar knot in my stomach as my mind went into *What can I do to fix this?* mode. I was sinking into that bog of forgetfulness of who I am and who God is, when I finally told myself *stop*, and reached for the wonderful wisdom in Proverbs 3:5–7 (MSG):

Trust God from the bottom of your heart; don't try to figure out everything on your own. Listen for God's voice in everything you do, everywhere you go; he's the one who will keep you on track. Don't assume that you know it all. Run to God!

Don't you think that is so hard to do? I love to try to figure out things, but I know that I will never find peace and rest that way, because I am not in control.

Gideon, too, is very aware of this. For seven years, he's watched his family and friends go hungry at the hands of the Midianites. For seven years he's thought how defenseless his people are against their enemies. If Israel is to have any hope at all of even one square meal a day, Gideon knows they must hide to prepare it.

And so he is deep in the winepress when we meet him; it's here that he receives a strange visitor:

> One day the angel of GOD came and sat down under the oak in Ophrah that belonged to Joash the Abiezrite, whose son Gideon was threshing wheat in the winepress, out of sight of the Midianites. The angel of GOD appeared to him and said, "GOD is with you, O mighty warrior!" (Judges 6:11–12 MSG)

The Lord Is with You, Mighty Warrior!

I have heard many sermons about this passage and how the angel's words presented a kind of joke, as if God looked at a house cat and said, "I am with you, king of the forest!"

I don't hear the angel's words like that at all. I believe that when God looks at you right now he sees all of who you can be in his strength—and he addresses you as such.

For example, imagine that your marriage is in real trouble. There is such distance between you and your husband; words that remain unspoken and those you wish you had never said. You worry about your children and how the tension in the house affects them. You can't remember where things started to go wrong, but you feel as if you have gone too far to ever find your way back to each other. And then as you are praying one morning, an angel of the Lord appears beside you and addresses you, "The Lord is with you, beautiful daughter who saved and restored her family."

What?! You might be tempted to think, *That is just ridiculous.*

What we forget is that with God anything is possible, and he is known to use the least likely one to shine through, so that it is clear to all involved: *only God could have done this.*

Look at This Mess!

Of course Gideon's response to this idea, and to the angel, is so much like our own when we feel out of control. He momentarily ignores that "mighty warrior" salutation and tells the angel:

> If GOD is with us, why has all this happened to us? Where are all the miracle-wonders our parents and grandparents told us about, telling us, "Didn't GOD deliver us from Egypt?" The fact is, GOD has nothing to do with us—he has turned us over to Midian. (Judges 6:13 MSG)

Poor Gideon. He's desperate and tired, worn out from pounding so much wheat, his body taxed from laboring so hard to complete the work and remain on the lookout and run at even the hint of another raid. He's worried about an eighth year of little to eat, and frightened of letting even a single grain escape his attention. He pounds the golden stalks and pounds, and each strike is like a blow to his spirit, a bruise on his heart. He's sick of this and wonders *Where is God? Why isn't he helping us?*

Clearly Gideon hasn't heard what the prophets told Israel: that because they've not trusted God or obeyed him, then God has allowed them to see how things go when they trust themselves;

obviously that's not working so well. Or maybe Gideon's heard that message and is despairing and unsure of what to do. And it doesn't seem as if Gideon recognizes who's talking to him either. He is down in a winepress after all.

The angel turns closer to Gideon. Can't you can feel the benevolence in that move? The Scripture says the Lord looks at Gideon. You can see him zeroing in, kindly, closely, locking eyes. The Lord says: "Go in this strength that is yours. Save Israel from Midian. Haven't I just sent you?" (Judges 6:14 MSG). He is directive but also reassuring.

And maybe that is when Gideon thinks, *Wait a minute . . . who's talking here?*

In the Old Testament, the term "angel of the LORD" (with LORD in small caps, indicating the unspeakable name YHWH, or Yahweh) is always Christ himself; and his appearances are always life changing. For example, when the angel of the Lord appeared to Moses at the burning bush (Exodus 3:6), Moses hid his face because he was afraid to look at God. But just as that appearance triggered the Lord sending Moses to deliver his people, this appearance was sending Gideon to deliver Israel.

Life Changing?

Gideon must have sensed that what is happening to him is much bigger than he is, and you can see him teetering on the edge of taking a leap of faith here. . . .

But not quite yet. Gideon still wants some assurance. He's simply not certain that this is God. If this is God speaking, is he getting correctly what God wants? God, knowing what Gideon is feeling, offers comfort, like a handful of grain to the trust-hungry: *Peace. Do not fear. You shall live.*

Gideon builds an altar at the very spot where he almost gave in to his doubts and fears, his desire for control and urge to decide things for himself. And he calls the place where he's let his worries rest Jehovah Shalom.

The Lord is peace.

Time to Move

Now Gideon knows God has called him, and it's time to act, but how can he take on the whole Midianite nation? He doesn't know how to be a soldier. He's a wheat thresher.

God takes all the trust Gideon can muster and is gentle. *Let's take this a step at a time, Mighty Warrior*, he seems to say. *Let's begin to put things right for Israel by tackling what's going on in your own backyard first. See that altar to Baal and the Asherah pole? Tear down the altar, and use the pole as firewood to burn it all to the ground.*

You see, Israel had lost her way one more time in worshiping Baal and other false gods, and God tells Gideon to start cleaning house with his own father.

This is a terrifying assignment. Gideon's father, Joash, is a wealthy man and the sponsor of a large Baal cult site that includes an altar to Baal and an Asherah pole. (Asherah was supposed to be the wife of Baal or Baal's father, El.)

Gideon knows he could be killed for doing this, and he's probably wondering how this is going to address the Midianite problem.

This is where Gideon just has to trust. That trust is a good thing because God is showing Gideon that Israel's real problem isn't the Midianites stealing all their crops. The real issue is Israel's worship of false idols that is stealing all their souls.

Then, just as today, God wants our hearts. With our meager trust we often fail to see that. We look at the recession and identify that as causing our griefs. But Wall Street racing in and raiding our savings accounts, or snatching our harvests, isn't what's starving our souls. It's our idol worship, our fixation on things and status and comfort, and our distraction from heaven and God.

So God uses whatever he can to refocus our attention on him; it's not really new for him to see that he gets our attention when he uses external circumstances.

Gideon now has God's directions. He takes his father's prize bull to tear down the altar, and then he offers that bull as a sacrifice to God, using the Asherah pole as firewood. Next, Scripture tells us:

> Gideon selected ten men from his servants and did exactly what GOD had told him. But because of his family and the people in the neighborhood, he was afraid to do it openly, so he did it that night. (Judges 6:27 MSG)

In that one verse, that notable point that Gideon hurries and goes about this job at night, shows me that here is someone still used to grinding away in the winepress. Gideon wants to obey God, yet still is afraid, aware that he lives in a world of evil people who do evil things and he could get caught by them—maybe his own family. It's quite a sign of the times, isn't it, that Gideon knows that his people and even his own family will come after him for destroying a pagan altar rather than rallying behind him because he did the right thing? Trust, however, says: There are moments in life when it will cost you dearly to do what you know needs to be done—but look up. You'll see God sitting there, calling you by the name of the righteous person he knows you can be.

Of course this truth might not take away the scare of walking the edge of where trust leads, for by morning, Gideon sees his worst fears are realized:

The people in town were shocked to find Baal's altar torn down, the Asherah pole beside it chopped down, and the prime bull burning away on the altar that had been built. They kept asking, "Who did this?" Questions and more questions, and then the answer: "Gideon son of Joash did it." The men of the town demanded of Joash: "Bring out your son! He must die! Why, he tore down the Baal altar and chopped down the Asherah tree!" (Judges 6:28–30 MSG)

It's sad that in such a short period of history God's people have fallen so far away from where they started. In Deuteronomy 13, Moses told the people that if a relative or close friend even whispered about the possibility of worshiping a false god, they should be stoned. Now it's the one who destroys the false god's altar whose execution is demanded.

Gideon's father, however, is stirred by his son's courage. He doesn't chastise Gideon for taking away and offering up his prize bull to Yahweh, nor destroying the idols. In essence he says, "If this god needs us to defend him, he's not much of a god after all. Let him defend himself."

Whether it was Joash's statement that turned the tide, we're not told, but from that day on Gideon is given the nickname Jerub-baal: *Baal will contend against him.*

Gideon's Army

Now the Midianites, Amalekites, and all the sons of the east are furious that their gods are being mocked. They gather around Israel and prepare for the greatest raid ever.

Gideon understands the stakes and begins to live up to his name, both the name of the people and the name from the Lord.

Scripture next shows us the Mighty Warrior blowing a ram's horn, calling the different tribes of Israel to battle—the very ones who had just called for his execution.

What changed?

The key to this transformation is found in Judges 6:34: "GOD's Spirit came over Gideon" (MSG).

God's Spirit can transform any person—and whole nations. Gideon realizes this as he begins to live according to how God sees him. But the fact is Gideon is still the same man; even though God is going before him and a vast army of troops rallies in support behind him, Gideon is still uncertain about trusting God fully. He's learning how to trust, a step at a time, but he still has a lot of questions, mainly, does God always do what he says he will do?

Gideon still wrestles with that winepress mentality. He's still trying to pound out and gather salvation on an improvised threshing floor, instead of trusting the Spirit of God to blow through, separating all the right and good from the wrong.

So Gideon looks up and demands another sign from God—and not just once more, but twice.

A Blanket of Trust

You've heard fellow Christians, I'm sure, say, "I'm putting out a fleece" to seek what God wants on an issue. They may well be seeking God's will, but that's not what Gideon is doing in Judges 6:36–40.

Gideon already knows God's will for him—God's made that very clear, telling Gideon to strike the Midianites, with the promise that they will fall as if they were one man (6:16). So when Gideon asks God for a sign, he's really asking, *God, are you going to show up?*

I'm amazed at God's patience with Gideon and yet encouraged too. God doesn't treat his people as if they are all alike; he knows each one of our hearts and treats us accordingly. Gideon, God knows, needs some encouragement.

So God turns toward Gideon and leans in and looks his mighty warrior straight in the eye. And Gideon says, "I'll put this fleece out all night, God—on the threshing floor—and if in the morning the fleece is covered with dew but the threshing ground around it is dry, then I'll know that you will indeed deliver Israel through me."

And God answers Gideon's call for a signal; the next morning, the fleece is soaked and the threshing ground around it is bone dry. Gideon is even able to squeeze from the fleece a whole bowl of water. But he's still not fully convinced. *What if this is just my imagination, or some pipedream to want to conquer my enemies? What if this is not God at all?* Gideon's so uncertain. He asks God not to be angry with him, but could he try this experiment just one more time, only the other way around—wet threshing ground, dry fleece?

God is gracious. A second time he shows up on the threshing floor, this time leaving the ground soaked and the fleece completely dry.

Gideon is suddenly sure and resolved, with no mistake: *God is here and I am ready to go.*

I find God's patience here so encouraging—and truly it is loving patience. He doesn't expect you or me to leap from overwhelmed woman to overcoming warrior. No, he takes us one step at a time along shores of trust.

Trust Me!

There are themes that flow from the first page of God's Word to the end, and one of the most prevalent is this call to trust him with all we are and all we have. God hungers for our love and trust. He proves himself over and over, and still we tend to doubt that he is with us. With the battle against the Midianites ahead, God wants to show his people one more time that they can trust him and not be afraid, so he decides to reduce Gideon's army to the size of a large choir.

Gideon starts out the day with an army of thirty-two thousand men; God tells Gideon to allow any of them who are afraid to leave. Twenty-two thousand men turn and run. I can't imagine the look on Gideon's face as he watches more than two-thirds of his army head home to their moms.

However, he still has ten thousand men, a respectable number.

But God sees that is still too many. He tells Gideon to take the men down to the river and watch how they drink the water. Whoever scoops a drink with his hands can stay; but whoever gets down on his knees and laps the water like a dog is to be sent home.

Nine thousand and seven hundred men get down on their knees, and Gideon is left with just three hundred men.

That's quite a reduction: from thirty-two thousand soldiers to just three hundred. This must have seemed insane to Gideon. *Why on earth*, he must have wondered, *would God reduce the numbers so drastically that I'm left with a group more the size of a church choir than an invading army?*

God hears the self-talk Gideon is giving himself. So that night he tells Gideon that if he is still afraid, he should creep down to the enemy camp with Purah, his right-hand man, and listen to what's being said.

If he is still afraid! Gideon is terrified, so he and Purah make their way toward the enemy camp. Now you know Gideon can't even begin to count the number of troops, for they are like locusts carpeting the land; as they creep closer, they hear two men having a conversation about a dream one had just had. The man says he dreamed a loaf of bread rolled into a Midianite tent and flattened it to the ground. The other man interprets the dream for him, "This has to be the sword of Gideon son of Joash, the Israelite! God has turned Midian—the whole camp!—over to him" (Judges 7:14 MSG).

This Had to Be God!

Have you ever found yourself in a situation where there was no doubt that God is involved? This conversation that Gideon and Purah overhear has to take the cake—literally. The dream itself seems innocuous. There is nothing in the image of a large loaf of barley bread hitting a tent and the tent falling over to suggest that victory belonged to Gideon and his troops. But the interpretation is almost comical.

First, how on earth would this Midianite soldier even know Gideon's name?

Second, why would he not interpret the tent as being one belonging to the Israelites, whom they have been successful in rousting for the past seven years? This is clearly God saying to Gideon, *Hello? Can you hear me now? I am with you!*

Finally Gideon gets it. He returns to his troops and announces that God has already won the battle for them. He divides his troops into three groups of one hundred men, and they set out toward the Midianites' camp, armed with . . . trumpets, empty jars, and torches.

These are not exactly the weapons of war, which is the whole point: God's ways are not our ways. When we try to figure out things on our own, we will fail; when we trust him and follow him no matter how things seem to us or those around us, there is amazing victory.

Victory in God's Name

So the Israelite troops march upon the Midianites and Amalekites and all the enemies of the east. They blow their trumpets, smash the jars, and hold up their torches, crying out, "A sword for the Lord and for Gideon!"

The great irony of the cry is not one man in the whole group is carrying a sword . . . at least not to the human eye. Instead of iron, steel, or metal, they carry the truth and trust that God is with them; the sword of the Spirit is living, breathing, defeating to whoever stands against God and his people. The Midianite troops cannot stand against such truth, such trust in God. They turn on one another in confusion, slaughtering each other. Only a remnant escape back toward the desert, where even they are eventually destroyed.

Gideon's story tells me a lot about myself and even more about God.

God chose an unlikely young man to prove to his people that he was, is, and always will be with them. The simple yet profound lesson from Gideon is that it's all about God. The story is really not about Gideon; the story is about our Father.

As I think of the days that we live in, I take two great truths from the days of Gideon.

One, the problem was never the Midianites; the problem was that God's people turned away from him and began worshiping false gods. When we find ourselves in hard times, peace will only be found in our Father's arms.

Second, as we grow in faith and trust, it's a huge mistake to think, *Well, now I am really strong, I've really got a handle on this.* The truth is that we are learning more and more that God can be trusted. The strongest place to rest is in an understanding that we can do nothing apart from Christ. That is trust and that is the place where I take all my fear.

I find great beauty in this truth as a wife, mother, speaker, and author. Perhaps you want to be a better wife and you try so hard to do it on your own. Some days are good and on others you fall flat on your face. The temptation is to pat yourself on the back for the "good" days and berate yourself for the others. I've been there. But God does not ask us to be good wives and mothers. He asks us to trust him, turn to him, lean in to him, follow his call and his heart. It is Christ who makes us beautiful.

When I stepped off the stage at the first Women of Faith conference, I was shaking (and leaking—it was time to feed my newborn son Christian again!)—maybe out of relief, in part, but more out of feeling overwhelmed by the response of the women who had graciously stood to their feet when I finished my story. After I had taken care of Christian and he was napping, I stepped out to the book table for a few moments to sign some books.

A woman in her forties took my hand in hers and said, "You are living my dream."

I asked her what she meant by that.

"God put a dream in my heart to do just what you are doing," she replied, "but it was fifteen years ago. I've been waiting all this time. When you said at the beginning of your talk that you were scared and didn't feel ready, I wanted to shout, 'I'm ready! I've been ready and waiting for fifteen years. What has God done with my dream?'"

I didn't have an answer for her question, but I knew someone who had been where she was and asked the very same thing.

NINE

Trusting God
with Your Dreams

The Beauty of Forgiving

Nothing is as real as a dream. The world can change around
you, but your dream will not. Responsibilities need not erase
it. Duties need not obscure it. Because your dream is within
you, no one can take it away.

—Tom Clancy

Joseph had a dream. When he told it to his brothers,
they hated him even more.

—Genesis 37:5 msg

Recently I was packing for a weekend in Connecticut where I would take part in a Friday night worship concert, a women's conference on Saturday, and three Sunday services with their pastor. The pastor, Clive Calver, is my former boss from British Youth for Christ. I became a youth evangelist with Youth for Christ when I was twenty-three years old, and though my immediate boss in the music department was worship leader and songwriter Graham Kendrick, Clive was head of BYFC and very involved with nurturing his staff. Memories of my time working for him came flooding back to me.

One event in particular stood out above all others, only I hoped Clive had forgotten about it. The event happened during a tour that he, Graham, our worship band, and I took part in from one end of England to the other.

Each evening, Graham and I led in worship, and Clive preached. As the tour progressed, Clive's messages seemed to get longer and longer and longer. It was our habit to eat after the event, so most evenings we were starving, just waiting for Clive to say that blessed word: "Amen!"

One night I was feeling particularly restless. Clive had been speaking for forty-five minutes, and there wasn't even a whiff of an "amen" on the horizon. I wandered outside the venue and found a sweet little dog without a collar that seemed to be a stray. I played with it for a while and then, when it began to rain, brought it inside. I took the dog backstage and gave it some water and a sandwich. Then I sat with the dog at the side of the stage, listening to Clive. The dog appeared interested, even seemed open to going on and participating in the program. I held on to it for a moment knowing that I was about to do something ill-advised and inappropriate, but then I thought, *Oh, why not!*

I let it go and the dog walked onto the stage and stood looking out at the audience. Clive was at the front of the stage and had no idea what was unfolding behind him. The dog wandered around for a little while and then proceeded to relieve himself on a plant, part of the stage scenery (I guess I gave him too much water). Most of the people in the audience were falling off their chairs in laughter.

Finally the dog went up to Clive and sat beside him, obviously hoping they could finish the message together.

I still cannot believe that Clive didn't fire me on the spot!

Well, it had been twenty-five years since we had worked together, and I was looking forward to catching up on what had been happening in his life and with his family. What I couldn't have anticipated was how Clive would touch my life with a memory of his own that had nothing to do with stray dogs or irreverent employees.

That weekend, as Clive, his wife Ruth, Barry, Christian, and I had dinner, he gave me a very unusual gift. He let me know that thirty years ago, a man whom I loved and trusted saw a dream that God had placed in my life when no one else did. This man understood something that has taken me a lifetime to learn: that when God places a dream in your heart, it may take years to come to pass, but you can trust his timing.

A Wonderful Man

That man who saw the dream in me was Clive's father-in-law, Gilbert Kirby, one of the most influential people in my life. Dr. Kirby was president of the London School of Theology when I was a student there, and he was wise and kind and very funny. His wife, Connie, was a charming hostess who would invite the new students in groups of ten to come over to their lovely home on campus and have tea with them.

I was running late for my tea date and, realizing this was very bad form, I attempted to hurry—never wise if you are me. The Kirbys' front door was open when I got to their home, and I could hear the other students inside, laughing and talking. I knocked a couple of times and then went in; Mrs. Kirby rose from her chair as I entered the parlor and extended her hand to me, and in my usual graceful way I fell over her dog and landed flat on my face at her feet.

I would love to tell you that the pup I tripped over was a tiny, three-pound Yorkie, but it was a one-hundred-pound Labrador named F. F. Bruce after the great biblical history scholar.

So much for making a good impression.

Thank goodness the Kirbys saw beyond my clumsy trips and falls, for several weeks later I would find myself invited by Dr. Kirby to sit by the fire as his secretary brought us a cup of tea. (Nothing in Britain can be resolved without the presence of tea.)

This was after quite a journey at seminary, however. You see, I had decided to go to seminary, believing with all my heart and soul that God had called me to share his love with others around the world. I had known this since I was seventeen years old, when, as part of a crowd of twenty thousand young people I had responded to a call from Dr. Billy Graham to set my life apart for God's service. I had packed my bags and got on the train from Glasgow, Scotland, to London to take the next step, believing that God wanted me to train for becoming a missionary to India. But after about six months of church history and theology classes and lectures, I was through with seminary. I decided that I was wasting my time learning about the reformation of the sixteenth century when people all around me were starving and going to hell.

I was then convinced it was my responsibility to let Dr. Kirby know. I thought he might want to commission me and send me off to India after a short but meaningful service in front of the student body, which of course would be humbled by my passion. So I made an appointment through his secretary and waited for my time with anticipation.

When the day came, Dr. Kirby listened very carefully as I passionately presented my case and my call. With a few gentle, well-chosen words, he helped me see that perhaps this was God's time to prepare me for whatever plan he had for my life.

He told me, "God is more interested in what he is doing in you than through you."

I'd never thought of that before. I left Dr. Kirby's office grateful for his counsel but sure that the minute I was out of ear-shot he'd be calling one of the other professors to say, "Guess what I just heard from that character from north of the border!"

Since that fireside chat I've thought back on what Dr. Kirby said. He had been very gracious with me, and I'd been foolish and arrogant. *What must this dear man have thought of me?*

More than thirty years later, sitting at dinner in a noisy restaurant in Connecticut, Dr. Kirby's daughter Ruth would answer my very question.

"I adored your father," I told Ruth. "He was always so kind and patient with me."

"He loved you too," she said. "I remember once when you were singing in chapel, Dad called me and said, 'You have to come and hear this girl. God has such a plan for her life.'"

"When was that?" I asked.

"You were a second-year student at the time," she recalled.

If Ruth had given me a gift-wrapped Shetland pony, I couldn't have been happier. I thought that all Dr. Kirby had seen was a silly girl who was out of touch with reality, but instead he saw my heart and recognized the dream and the call. I just had no idea how strange the path would look that would take me there.

What About You?

What has happened to your dreams? Does it seem as if they have been buried beneath a busy life, or do you question yourself as to whether they ever had any validity at all? Do you doubt they will ever come true? Do you trust God for their timing?

I think back to the words of my wise mentor Dr. Kirby: *Jesus is more interested in what he is doing in you than through you.*

In our humanity we have timetables in our hearts and, when our life veers away from those, we assume that we are off course or we have missed whatever it was God had for us at one point. I no longer believe that to be true. All we are asked to do is to trust God and keep following him, no matter how dark the path gets. Surely no life illustrates that more clearly than that of Joseph.

Broken Dreams

To understand Joseph, it helps to take a brief look at Jacob, his father, a man who had known a lot of conflict and spent much of his life on the run.

Jacob is a cheater, who schemes his brother Esau out of his birthright and their father's blessing, and fears the day he ever has to meet Esau again, face-to-face. But Jacob also tastes the bitterness of betrayal himself at the hand of his uncle, a man for whom he works seven years. He's labored with the promise of marrying Laban's daughter Rachel. But after the wedding ceremony, on their wedding night, when the veil is lifted, Jacob finds he has been tricked into marrying Rachel's older sister Leah.

This is not the woman he loves and has been promised. His dream is shattered.

Even though Leah eventually gives Jacob six sons and a

daughter, I don't think it ever leaves her mind that he was tricked into marrying her; I don't imagine that made him an easy man to live with either.

Jacob, meanwhile, schemes with Laban on how to realize his dream of marrying Rachel, whom he adores. Jacob and Laban wheel and deal, and Jacob and Rachel do marry, but they encounter another broken dream because she isn't able to have children.

So Rachel is jealous of the children Leah has been able to give Jacob, and Leah knows that Rachel has Jacob's heart, and this is a family in conflict.

Then one day: "God remembered Rachel. God listened to her and opened her womb. She became pregnant and had a son. She said, 'God has taken away my humiliation.' She named him Joseph" (Genesis 30:22–24 MSG). So now Rachel has everything: the love of her husband, and the joy of giving him a son.

You have to know this is a bitter blow to Leah, and I'm sure she talked to her boys about it.

The Favored Son

It's into this world and home divided that Joseph bursts—Joseph, the long-awaited, beloved son.

Now Rachel becomes pregnant one more time and has one more son. But she dies in childbirth.

Imagine the Jacob household now: if it was hard to compete with a wife who is more loved than you have ever been, just imagine what it's like to compete with a dead one who with her last breath delivers one more son to the husband who adores her.

It is clear to everyone that Joseph has a very special place in Jacob's heart, and Joseph doesn't wear that lightly:

The story continues with Joseph, seventeen years old at the time, helping out his brothers in herding the flocks. These were his half brothers actually, the sons of his father's wives Bilhah and Zilpah. And Joseph brought his father bad reports on them. Israel loved Joseph more than any of his other sons because he was the child of his old age. And he made him an elaborately embroidered coat. When his brothers realized that their father loved him more than them, they grew to hate him—they wouldn't even speak to him. (Genesis 37:2–4 MSG)

Joseph just asks for trouble, doesn't he? It's one thing to know that you are your father's favorite, but it's another to flaunt it and quite another to blacken your brothers' reputations.

Every boy needs to know that he is loved and approved of by his father, and that need seems to remain well into manhood. I remember being introduced to a very successful businessman after a lunch where I had been the guest speaker. As we talked, he told me that one of the greatest wounds in his life was that he never won his father's approval. I could see in his eyes that even after all the years that had passed and the success that he had created, the wound remained.

Every one of Jacob's sons must have felt this way too.

Reuben was Jacob's firstborn son, but he was not the favored one. Dan was the first son born from Rachel's maid, Bilhah, but he also was not the favorite. Joseph was the golden boy—and they all knew it.

The Gift Before the Receiver

Joseph not only had his father's love but a God-given gift, the ability to interpret dreams. It's notable that God doesn't wait until Joseph is mature enough to handle the gift of interpreting dreams. The gift is in place before Joseph has the wisdom or grace to know how to use it:

> Joseph had a dream. When he told it to his brothers, they hated him even more. He said, "Listen to this dream I had. We were all out in the field gathering bundles of wheat. All of a sudden my bundle stood straight up and your bundles circled around it and bowed down to mine." His brothers said, "So! You're going to rule us? You're going to boss us around?" And they hated him more than ever because of his dreams and the way he talked. (Genesis 37:5–8 MSG)

If that's not foolish, I wouldn't recognize foolish if it sat up in my porridge wearing a kilt! Why did Joseph share this dream with his brothers? No one asked him about it, this wasn't a dream that needed interpreting, and he had to know this would make his already-jealous brothers even more so.

Young Joseph, however, obviously enjoyed the thought that someday his brothers would bow down before him. What he didn't count on was how far that was in the future and what a long, hard road it would be before he got there.

You can't chalk this mistake up to Joseph's youth—that he just didn't know better. Contrast his insensitivity to the grace and maturity of Mary, the mother of Jesus. Mary was a young teenager when she was visited by an angel and told she would be the mother of the coming Messiah. We are told that on several occasions she "pondered these things in her heart." There was no sense of entitlement but rather gentle humility. Can you imagine Mary walking around the market square in Nazareth saying, "Pleased to meet you. I am about to be the mother of the Savior of the world, but you can call me Mary." No, Mary knew, if not from instruction then intuitively, to keep certain information close to her heart—to think on how her words and actions would affect others.

Pushing the Limits

Joseph, on the other hand, apparently learns nothing from the negative response from his brothers. So when he receives another dream, he decides to share it again, this time not only with his brothers but his father too.

Now Jacob is angry with Joseph, who tells him that his latest dream includes his own father bowing down to him.

I wonder, at this point, if Jacob looks back on his own life and realizes he, too, has learned nothing from his parents' mistakes. He's had a lifetime to think about how his father loved his brother Esau best (Genesis 25:28), while his mother, Rebekah, favored him; and how his mother helped him cheat his brother out of his blessing. It took an entire generation to reunite the families.

Yet here Jacob is again, causing—and seeing his son cause— the same kind of tension that can lead to disaster.

Did he know that when disaster is on the horizon, you can trust that God is still in control?

Who Do You Think You Are?

Step back for a minute and think of Joseph at this point. Surely he's seeing how all his sharing is stirring up his family. But perhaps he's feeling a little wounded here too. He's shared not one but two dreams, and instead of his family engaging in what they hear and pondering with him what it all means, they're criticizing him, picking apart the very dream.

This had to be devastating.

Have you ever shared what you believe God has called you to, trusting that the one(s) you share with will care about the dream as much as you do—only they haven't. They've laughed or put down your even having the dream? Perhaps you've shared a dream with your family, expecting that they would encourage you, but instead they try to crush your dream and maybe you too. Perhaps they haven't spoken these words, but they are palpable: "Who do you think you are?"

The truth is that it doesn't matter who you think you are, because God knows who you are; and when he puts his hand on a human heart, the rest is up to him.

It's easy to doubt a dream, to get discouraged when the signs of a dream's fulfillment are not apparent or even possibly on the horizon. It's easy, when God calls, to imagine he'll put a path before us that's clear from one point to the next—that there will be an obvious unfolding of that plan in ways that make sense. But that is usually not the way things happen. Many dreams lie beyond a fog that we must wander through, and they often take us on detours that require trust in God to get back on course.

And this was certainly the case for Joseph.

The First Dark Night

After hearing this latest dream, Joseph's brothers decide they've had enough. Once more they've heard how they will someday all bow down to and serve their brother Joseph. It's time, they decide, to get rid of their pesky brother once and for all.

So when they see Joseph headed their way one day, Genesis 37:18–20 tells how they mutter to one another: *Look, here comes the dreamer.* And they cook up a plan to kill their brother.

We only know what was going on in the hearts of the brothers because of what Moses, the author of Genesis, writes for us, and some of this is between the lines. Joseph's younger brother, Benjamin, is just a little boy so he is at home; but the other ten brothers watch Joseph approach. One of the brothers suggests throwing Joseph in a pit and saying a wild animal has eaten him—and one just might, had Joseph been left at the mercy of the wild. Nine of the boys want to kill Joseph, but Reuben, the eldest, intervenes.

Reuben tells his brothers that he won't tolerate murder and doesn't even want to shed any of Joseph's blood . . . but they could throw Joseph in an open well.

Fair enough, the brothers agree. A pit? A well? Either way, Joseph would be out of the picture—and their hair.

Moses lets us know that Reuben intends to go back at night, rescue Joseph, and return him to their father. Reuben wants to do the right thing, just not enough to stand up to his brothers, to trust that God is in control; that decision will cost Joseph, Reuben, and, perhaps most of all, Jacob.

As for Joseph, you have to wonder what went on in his mind as he lay bruised and devastated at the bottom of the well. Did he let anger and hatred for his brothers burn inside him? Did he fix upon grief that they hated him so? Did he think tenderly on his past and his father, perhaps recalling the stories—full of irony now—of how his grandfather, Isaac, was blessed by digging a series of wells like this very one he's been thrown into (Genesis 26:18–33)? Did he question his role in all this, maybe even his dreams? Did he think his brothers had just changed the course of his life and destroyed whatever plans God had for him?

What happens to you when you find yourself at the bottom of a well with no warning? Do you think your life is over? Do you believe that God's will for you has been thwarted?

I trust with everything in me that God is bigger than any scheme of man! God uses even the things that someone intends for harm to make something beautiful—to make us more like Jesus.

Maybe you have been thrown into a pit by force, or maybe it's a pit of your own choosing because of these times we live in. Certainly we face tremendous financial uncertainty, and people are losing jobs and homes and having to start over in ways no one could ever imagine. But these things are not new. They happened centuries ago, and Joseph's story shows what can happen when you trust that God is at work—regardless if he has to pull you from a pit you were forced into or chose (even if unwittingly).

You see, instead of being rescued by Reuben at midnight, Joseph is taken from that pit and sold as a slave to Midianite traders headed to Egypt.

A New Day

In Egypt, Joseph is sold into slavery to Potiphar, an Egyptian who is captain of Pharaoh's guard. It would seem that this is the beginning of his end, right? But there is a very telling verse in Genesis 39:2: "God was with Joseph" (msg).

The fact that God is with Joseph doesn't stop his brothers from betraying him. No, there is no supernatural intervention that rescues him from the Midianites. God doesn't send an undercover envoy to purchase Joseph at the slave market . . . but God is with him.

We tend to think that if God is with us, things will fall into place in ways that make us feel comfortable and safe. That is what trust in God procures, right?

Not at all. The logic is not: trust God and he will always keep you safe. Bad things—frightening things!—happen every day to those who love the Lord. The truth is: what makes us safe is the absolute truth that God is with us no matter what our circumstances.

This is not an easy truth to know; I have to say, some of this feels new to me. If you had asked me earlier in my Christian walk, "Do you believe that God is in control of your life?" I would have said yes. Slowly, however, I'm getting a bigger picture of what that looks like.

Joseph's story shows me how God will use whatever it takes to help us understand that all we need now, or have ever needed, is him—and he is with us. You see, Joseph doesn't seem to have been very aware of this truth either. We don't hear much that he was ever aware of his need for God, or that God had always been with him . . . until he is in a foreign country as a slave, with no rights, no ability to choose his own way to go.

Circumstance can often be the wind that brings us right back to the throne of grace. And it's here, in Egypt, when Joseph can no longer trust himself, that we see him begin to trust God.

Punished for Doing the Right Thing

In the next few years Joseph works very hard for Potiphar, eventually gaining enough trust to be put in charge of all Potiphar's personal affairs.

We don't hear Joseph pray any particular prayer or see any single moment of turning toward God, but obviously that is happening. We know because Potiphar himself recognizes that God is with Joseph (Genesis 39:3), and Potiphar, with respect, even uses the Hebrew word for God, *Yahweh*. Now *Yahweh* was God's special name, revealed only to his people. Potiphar would never have known that name unless Joseph had told Potiphar of this God he loved and who was with him.

So, as Joseph serves Potiphar, he might begin to think that the worst is behind him—because, true, he's suffered and been abandoned by his family, mocked for his dreams, and betrayed. But he has worked hard and now has a new life in a new place, far away from those who want to hurt him.

And yet is it?

The next chapter of Joseph's life is hard to process. Here we are allowed to see that even when we do the right thing because we love and trust God, he does not always protect us from the lies of others or the consequences of those lies. For in Potiphar's palace, Potiphar's wife tries over and again to seduce Joseph. Each time she tries, Joseph resists her advances, stating his devotion to God and respect for her husband.

But, as William Congreve wrote in *The Mourning Bride*, "Hell hath no fury like a woman scorned."

And Potiphar's wife feels scorned, indeed. Humiliated, probably out of her guilt and shame. So she accuses Joseph of trying to rape her. She wants to remove the person she claims has humiliated her, and in her accusation, humiliates her husband in front of his staff.

"The Hebrew slave, the one you brought to us," she says, "came after me and tried to use me for his plaything" (Genesis 39:17 MSG).

The language she uses for "Hebrew slave" is a strong racial slur, and the implication to her husband is, "You are the one who brought this trash into our home."

Joseph is thrown into prison. But the fact that he is not executed is unmistakable evidence that Potiphar is not convinced that his wife is telling the truth. If Potiphar had really believed that a foreign slave had attempted to rape his wife, he would have executed, on the spot, the would-be rapist. Instead, and probably because all his servants are watching, Potiphar has to do something, so prison becomes a good solution, a holding place, till he can sort out everything.

Doesn't this seem to fly in the face of everything you have been raised to believe in our Western evangelical culture?

Here is a young man who (finally) honors God in a pagan household. He's become a positive witness to his Lord. And he's resisted the advances of a seductive woman when no one else is watching. Who would have known, anyway, if he'd given in to Potiphar's wife? Joseph is a virile young man, in a foreign country, and a beautiful woman is trying to lure him into her bed. But he says no because it is the right thing to do; it's one thing to resist temptation because you think you might get caught, and quite another when you resist because you love God. Despite all this, Joseph is thrown in jail! God even allows Potiphar's wife to grab evidence as he runs away from her. So with his robe in her hand and her word against that of a slave, Joseph is doomed.

Taken to a Prison to Be Set Free

You would think that Joseph might be frustrated here with God, ready to take back his trust that God is going to make his dreams happen. Yet even after Joseph is unfairly imprisoned, he still trusts and obeys God. He still demonstrates integrity.

We read, "There in jail GOD was still with Joseph . . . The head jailer put Joseph in charge of all the prisoners—he ended up managing the whole operation." (Genesis 39:21, 22 MSG).

I feel a peculiar affinity to Joseph at this point in his life. I don't mean for a moment to compare spending one month in a psychiatric hospital with years in a prison, but I laughed when I read that Joseph was put in charge of the other prisoners. I had a similar experience. There is something very liberating about coming to terms with where you are, because you know that no matter how things appear to others, God is with you. I learned this when I had been in the hospital just a couple of weeks and the other patients made me the entertainment secretary. It had been a shock to my system to go from being a television talk-show host to a patient in the locked ward of a psychiatric hospital. So when I accepted the secretary role, I had to come to terms with my new reality. I took my job very seriously and tried to find ways to help so many of my new, broken friends, even for just a moment. In the process, the other patients became my new community and one I learned to love. And this is the way of trust: accepting and learning to love enough that you just know God has a plan, some way of working things for the good.

Joseph is believing that. He is winning the respect and trust of the jailer and being given free rein because at last Joseph has become trustable. He is trustable because of whom he trusts. And in the process, two things happen: He experiences more freedom than most people on the outside enjoy. And Joseph is being changed. He is beginning again to dream dreams. Only now he is a different man than the arrogant seventeen-year-old boy who came to Potiphar's palace because he enjoyed flaunting his gift in front of his brothers.

In his wonderful and insightful book *God Meant It for Good*, Dr. R. T. Kendall writes, "Every trial is designed to show you something about yourself that you did not know."[1] I have thought long and hard about that statement, especially in regard to a time when I was betrayed by someone I loved and trusted. Didn't that trial teach me something about the other person—a revealing of their true nature—and not something about me?

The truth is every trial, and my response to it, reveals

something more about me because it forces me to answer, with either my heart and mind or my behavior:

- I say I trust God, but do I?
- I say God is in control, but will I let go?
- I say God is my deliverer, but will I allow him to vindicate me?
- I say God is my defender, but do I still want to speak up for myself?

And the answers to these kinds of questions? Well, like John Cotton, the highly respected minister among the New England Puritans, was quoted as saying, "As long as there's a wriggle left in you, you're not ready."[2]

Not Yet, Joseph

Now it just happens that two members of Pharaoh's staff, the head butler and baker, end up in prison along with Joseph. And the captain of the guard has put Joseph in charge of them to take care of their needs.

One night, both the butler and baker have dreams that trouble them. It is touching here that, even though Joseph is a prisoner too, he is not only focused on his own circumstances. He notices when others are troubled and he tries to help.

The butler and baker tell Joseph about their dreams, and for the first time we see Joseph use the gift he once flaunted for his own sake for the good of others. He carefully listens to his fellow prisoners and then shares that he is able to interpret the dreams.

One dream is good news, he tells the butler: you will be

restored to service within three days. The other is terrible news, he consoles the baker: Within three days, you will be executed.

Dr. Kendall's book *God Meant It for Good* makes an interesting observation here about Joseph's parting words to the butler, "Only remember me when things are going well with you again—tell Pharaoh about me and get me out of this place" (Genesis 40:14 MSG). Dr. Kendall asserts that this plea of Joseph's kept him in prison for two more years. He writes, "God wanted to teach Joseph a deeper lesson: that God could do it utterly without Joseph's help."[3]

So maybe, though Joseph is changing, he still has much to learn about trusting God. Or maybe it is just a case of human nature because of course the butler, upon release from prison, forgets all about Joseph. And Joseph does indeed spend two more years in prison until one night Pharaoh himself has a dream.

Now no one seems able to interpret Pharaoh's dream; this is when the butler remembers Joseph.

So Joseph is brought from the prison into Pharaoh's presence; for the first time, we hear Joseph making it clear that he has no power in himself to interpret this dream but that God is the one who reveals the interpretation. It is a stunning point. Joseph is walking the way of trust.

So he listens to Pharaoh carefully—prayerfully, you can imagine—and he receives from God an interpretation.

Pharaoh is so impressed by this now thirty-year-old man, that he makes Joseph prime minister of Egypt. Even more extraordinary: Joseph gets a new Egyptian name, Zaphenath-Paneah, and Egyptian though it may be, look at its meaning: "God speaks and he lives!"

God speaks and he lives. Even in Egypt. Even in the dreams of butlers and bakers and kings. Even in a prisoner now made prime minister.

What if you were to sit down with Joseph today? Would you tell him that you feel as if God has lost your address? That you have waited and waited, and it still seems as if God is doing nothing to bring you out of the dark prison you find yourself in, through no choice of your own? That you have tried to help him out at times, and that hasn't worked out so well?

I imagine Joseph, prime minister of Egypt, might look you in the eye and say, "You are not forgotten. God sees you. In his perfect time, you will see him do what only he can do."

Who Is in Control?

You see, somewhere in this period of Joseph's life, he has totally forgiven his brothers. We see this when a terrible famine brings them to the prime minister of Egypt. The prime minister controls all the grain in the land, and Jacob, now old and ailing, sends his sons to ask for food because their family is starving.

Imagine the picture as the ten brothers stand before Joseph. Though it's been some twenty years, he recognizes them. They, however, do not see Joseph in the face of the prime minister, the second most powerful man in all of Egypt. They don't make the connection at all; they probably had no idea that Joseph was even still alive.

How tempting for Joseph to see his brothers there, begging from him, and want to remind them of his dream long ago—the dream in which they would be bowing down to him. How much he might have wanted to make them pay for mocking him, throwing him into a well, abandoning him to death—or as it turned out, slavery—all those years ago.

There is a breathless moment when Joseph reveals himself, and his brothers are understandably terrified. Will their now-powerful brother have them executed on the spot?

Joseph surprises them. He tells them he has no desire for revenge. But could he see his father?

Knowing Who Holds Your Dream

It has been more than twenty years since Jacob and Joseph have seen each other, and their father-son reunion is undeniably emotional. Joseph was Jacob's favorite son; you wonder, did he have Rachel's eyes or laugh? Did Jacob look at Joseph and hold on to him remembering the wife he loved and worked for so long but lost too soon? And Joseph: how long he must have yearned for the embrace of the father who thought he could do no wrong and loved him most, with all he had.

You can imagine that even Pharaoh must have been moved, seeing the two together.

Pharaoh tells Joseph to give his family whatever they need. They are welcome in Egypt, he says, and may even settle with their flocks in Goshen, the most fertile land available.

The family of Jacob and Joseph are blessed and reunited. But the brothers still expect the other shoe to drop. Even though they have received nothing but love and mercy from Joseph, they're not convinced that there won't be any consequences. *Maybe Joseph is waiting to exact his revenge when our father dies*, they must have wondered with one another. They had not been through the same refining process as Joseph.

So Jacob dies. His sons bury and mourn him.

And then Joseph's brothers send him a message, "Before his death, your father gave this command: Tell Joseph, 'Forgive your brothers' sin—all that wrongdoing. They did treat you very badly'" (Genesis 50:16–17 MSG).

When Joseph receives the message, he weeps. I think he weeps because he realizes that after all these years, after all the goodness given in Egypt, after all the ways he's tried to show, not just tell, that he has changed—his brothers have not really changed at all. They still have a revenge mentality. They still assume Joseph will do to them what they themselves would do in his position. They are living in a pit and prison of distrust, while he has been set free.

Can't you hear what Joseph longs to tell his brothers: When you finally understand that God is in control of everything, you don't have to hold grudges or be bitter and unforgiving. If you really trust God with your dreams, you can say, "You meant evil against me; but God meant it for good" (Genesis 50:20).

Learning to trust God totally transformed Joseph from an arrogant, self-confident boy into a man whose heart was tender, forgiving, and free. I find it encouraging that God's criteria for using a person is not that he or she has a great beginning, as Joseph did, but that God sees what is possible and patiently works through the years to refine and peel away the layers of selfishness.

Think about your own life right now. Perhaps you started out with a dream of what you believed God would do with your life. Then life itself got in the way. Maybe even at this moment, you sit wounded, broken, wondering where God is.

God is here. He is right here with you. He never left you but at every turn in the road longs to show you what is inside your heart and set you free. You are not a victim of the whims of others, no matter how true that may feel. You are a beloved daughter of the King who is making you into a person of greater and greater beauty as you learn to leave your dreams in his care.

That is the way of trust, true freedom; it is beautiful.

When Choices Cost Us Our Dreams

"That might be true for others," one woman said recently, "but not for me."

This woman and I met, each waiting in line to buy tickets for a movie. I'd asked her why she believed that what God offers to those who love him was not available to her too.

"Because I have destroyed everything that God ever gave me," she said. Then she asked me if I believed everything I wrote.

I told her that I did, but I didn't always live it out—I struggle too.

"I read your dream book," she said. *"God Has a Dream for Your Life."*

"What did you think?" I asked.

"I think that God does have a dream for each of us, but we can destroy it," she said.

I understood the kind of despair that makes someone believe this. "Do you think there's a place to start again," I asked, "even if you have made a mess of things?"

"Perhaps," she said. "Maybe in some situations." She paused. "Not in mine. My choices cost a lot of others their dreams too. If I could go back in time and redo things, I would. But it's too late for that."

My heart ached and I prayed for her as she paid for her ticket and said good-bye. It is a terrible weight to bear when you have brought down the walls of the house on those you love.

What I wished we'd had time to talk about is that I believe even in the rubble, there is hope.

TEN

Is It Ever Too Late to Start Again?

The Beauty of a Last Chance

A failure, within God's purpose, is no longer really a failure. Thus the cross, the supreme failure, is at the same time the supreme triumph of God, since it is the accomplishment of the purpose of salvation.

—PAUL TOURNIER

And Samson cried out to GOD: "Master, GOD! Oh, please, look on me again, Oh, please, give strength yet once more."

—JUDGES 16:28 MSG

Today as I write it is Mother's Day. Barry and I usually attend the second of two services at our church each Sunday, but as I had been invited to lead worship today I was up bright and early. Well, actually, I was just up early. Barry was gracious enough to drive to our neighborhood Starbucks and return with a bucket of caffeine as I dried my hair and we got out the door in time. I discovered that one of the huge benefits of arriving very early for our large church is that you can park without needing a packed lunch to make it from where you parked back to the main sanctuary.

Our music pastor told me that before my part of the service several babies would be dedicated. *Several* must be a Baptist word for *hordes*. It was like watching a baby-a-thon. Each family came forward with their little one and would pause for a moment to have their picture taken with our pastor. Some of the babies seemed quite happy to be there, others were asleep, and one was clearly not enamored with the whole process and had the lungs of a linebacker to express his feelings. It was quite a moving sight. One family had twin boys and another, girl triplets. The entire congregation seemed to wrap them up in a communal smile.

I was wearing a bracelet that Christian had given me that morning with the word *Mom* spelled out over and over again in small silver letters linked together. All in all, it was a lovely day for most of us, but I was very aware of a friend's absence that morning. It is simply too painful for her to be at a Mother's Day service. She is unable to have children of her own, and it is a wound that never closes. Having her in my life has made me aware that the things that bring many of us joy are like salt in an open sore to others. In those tender, raw places we can lose our way—and our trust.

The Wound Behind the Words

A couple of years ago I had one of my most dramatic encounters with a woman in all my years of traveling. I had finished speaking in an arena on the West Coast and was now signing books. She ignored my book signing line and cut to the front, getting decidedly in my space. If she had been any closer to me, she would have been me.

She said, "Why do you think we're all interested in your precious little stories about your perfect little son?"

"Trust me," I said, "he is far from perfect, and if I gave that impression then I'm sorry. He's just very loved."

"Well, I for one am sick of hearing about him!" she continued.

I could tell some of the women in my line were starting to get frustrated with her and were tossing in their own lines of support. I asked her if she wouldn't mind waiting for a few moments and then we could talk. When I was finished signing, I took her with me to a place where we could get a little privacy.

I asked her, "What happened to cause you this much pain?"

For a moment I actually thought she was going to hit me. Then she just seemed to fold in on herself. Her story is not mine to tell, but suffice to say she has lost children in unbelievably tragic ways. All I could do was hold her and weep with her.

There are no words for that depth of pain.

To be unable to give birth to a child has always been a peculiar heartache that is only understood by those who have been there or are there now. The rest of us can have great sympathy, but we don't really know how dark that night is.

In Old Testament times, inability to bear children was not only a heartache. It was a disgrace. To be unable to conceive was seen as a sign of God's disapproval, and a woman's worst nightmare. How could one trust him when feelings of such hope turn to pain and shame?

The Birth of Samson

There are so many stories in Scripture of those who had a wonderful beginning in God but lost their way, their hearts, and trust in the end.

Think of Lot. Once, he walked with Abraham but ended up drunk in a cave, committing incest with his daughters (Genesis 19). Lot's loss turned to debauchery. King Saul was the first king of Israel, a man the Spirit of God fell upon so profoundly that he was transformed. But Saul lost his ability to hear God's voice and took his own life after being critically wounded in battle (1 Samuel 31:4). Saul's loss turned to despair. In the New Testament, one of Paul's helpers, Demas, began serving God with fervor. Then the cost of following Christ seemed too high. In 2 Timothy 4, Paul writes that Demas deserted him because he loved the world too much. Demas's loss turned to isolation and separation.

In Judges 13:1, we read for the seventh time, "Again the Israelites did evil in the eyes of the LORD" (NIV). God's chosen ones, too, had lost their way.

But God, being God, feeling the depth of pain for his lost children, longs to hold his people; he waits and weeps and even is willing to use enemies to remind them of who he is and whose they are.

So for forty years God allowed the Philistines to oppress the Israelites, the longest oppression of his children recorded thus far in those first books of the Bible.

A woman trusting in him would change all that—she would bring hope to God's people and deliver them from their enemies.

She was a woman unable to conceive, who understood God's dark night, but we don't even know her name. Judges 13:2 tells us her husband's name was Manoah; she is only referred to as a sterile woman. There is something so sad about referring to her in that way, as if that was all you needed to know about her.

We do know she was chosen by God, since an angel of the Lord was sent to tell her:

> Even though you have been unable to have children, you will soon become pregnant and give birth to a son. So be careful; you must not drink wine or any other alcoholic drink nor eat any forbidden food. You will become pregnant and give birth to a son, and his hair must never be cut. For he will be dedicated to God as a Nazirite from birth. He will begin to rescue Israel from the Philistines. (Judges 13:3–5 NLT)

Manoah's wife accepts the news. She trusts in the message from God, and she runs to tell her husband. Imagine her joy: a baby! A son! A deliverer for all her people! But Manoah was overwhelmed by the very specific instructions: Hair never to be cut. Nazirite vows—and vows not just for a season and chosen on his own volition, as for most Nazirites, but for life, from first breath to last, from cradle to grave.

Certainly the strict regulations of the Nazirites, found in Numbers 6:1–21, would give anyone pause. Manoah, then, does what most of us do when faced with something startling. He wonders how and why and what. He worries. He doesn't think of what God does. He's concerned instead with the three main commitments of a Nazirite, how difficult they will be to sustain over a lifetime:

1. No cutting of the hair.

2. Abstinence from wine or strong drink and anything that grows on the vine.

3. No contact at all with the dead, even if it was your husband, wife, or child.

So Manoah is dubious, doubting, wanting to check out what his wife says she's heard from God. He's stewing and figuring, fretting and fidgeting. Manoah prays in his doubt for God to send the messenger again—he wants to check out the instructions for himself.

God understands doubt.

Again an angel appears to Manoah's wife, this time when she's sitting alone in a field. Again, she runs to tell her husband, who must see the messenger for himself.

Manoah peppers the stranger with questions: Are you the man who spoke to my wife (Judges 13:11)? If this comes to pass, what will become of my boy, what will he do (v. 12)? Can you stay—we'll grill some goat (v.15)?

Manoah's thinking this encounter requires more than a conversation. He's thinking, *Maybe if this messenger lingers, I can get to the bottom of all this.*

The angel is not fooled. He knows Manoah's wife trusts God's message. "Let the woman pay attention to all that I said" (v. 13 NASB), the angel says. "If you prepare a burnt offering, then offer it to the LORD" (v. 16 NASB).

Manoah, still not quite sure (v. 17), prepares the sacrifice. He asks the messenger his name. The angel tells Manoah his name is too wonderful to even utter. Glimmers of splendor begin to sparkle. Fires of trust start to flicker.

Manoah turns his attention to God; and when he sets the goat on the fire, offering a sacrifice to the one who sent good news, the angel ascends into the flame. It is a wonder, full of glory.

Manoah sees the miracle and begins to believe. He and his wife fall to the ground (v. 20). "We will surely die, for we have seen God" (v. 22 NASB), Manoah tells his wife.

Trust can do that to a person, she knows. She is on the ground with him. After there's nothing else you can do—when you finally accept that stewing and supposing and worrying don't lead to answers; when your heart faints and you are afraid of that dark night, and you can't figure it all out on your own, and everything seems to be going up in smoke—trust kicks in and knocks you to your knees.

A Promising Beginning

But the woman reminds her husband: as much as trusting can stun you or hurt, it doesn't kill you. For she has a promise—a son— and she isn't sure how this all will come to be, but she is willing to walk in trust a little longer.

So we see the woman of Judges 13 trusting. It's like God's promise is an irresistible tractor beam that has reached into her dark night of the soul and is drawing her to him. She gets up. So does Manoah. They begin this journey together. She gives birth to Samson, and she and Manoah raise him according to the Nazirite vows. Samson grows, and God blesses him (Judges 13:24).

Do you look at Samson's story and think, *What a great start?* Indeed, Samson seems to get all the breaks: green lights, clear road conditions, free parking, happy trails. His journey begins with the angel of the Lord predicting his birth. He has godly parents who love him. His life is dedicated to God's service. As a young man he experiences the power of God's Spirit.

But beginnings aren't everything. Trust isn't a destination.

Poets and preachers through the ages have reminded us that trust is simply the pathway to something greater—to God himself.

"Great is the art of beginning, but greater is the art of ending," wrote Henry Wadsworth Longfellow.

"I have fought the good fight," the apostle Paul proclaimed, "I have finished the race, I have kept the faith" (2 Timothy 4:7 ESV).

God knows, trust is a rocky road that will take even those with great beginnings through the dark.

The First Misstep

Samson's road takes him out of town, to Timnah—four miles into enemy territory. Did Samson realize he was in the land of the Philistines? Were his missteps intentional? Was he tired and enticed by an easier road? We don't know. But we do know he's depending on what he sees to get him somewhere. His decision is rash. He hasn't even spoken to the young woman he wants to marry. He simply sees her and trots home to persuade his parents to start arranging a wedding.

Is this what blind trust means?

Can't you hear that question lodged beneath what Samson's parents actually ask (Judges 14:3): *Can't you find a wife from your own land? Did you have to choose a wife from among our enemies?* There is pain in their voices. The girl, you see, is a Philistine. Her family is one of the oppressors of the Israelites.

Samson's reply is so much like ours when we look to fashion our own ways and figure our own plans: "Get her for me, for she looks good to me" (v. 3 NASB). Haven't you been there, or someone you know?

You're trying to get somewhere and you see things along that way that are enticing. Perhaps you open a credit card even though you promised you wouldn't, because you intend to just get this one thing you need and will pay it off straightaway. But one thing leads to another, and then to so much more.

Or you are having a hard time in your marriage and there's someone in your office who is kind and funny. You think, *What harm would there be in having lunch?* Before you can stop yourself, you are sharing yourself, heart and soul, if not body too, with someone else. You think, *As long as it's not a full-blown sexual relationship then I'm still on safe ground.* But Jesus said to trust God's way, and God's way requires more: "Don't think you've preserved your virtue simply by staying out of bed. Your *heart* can be corrupted by lust even quicker than your *body*. Those leering looks you think nobody notices—they also corrupt" (Matthew 5:28 MSG).

It's so easy to look in all the wrong places for our way through life. We want proofs and signs, paved paths. The road of trust isn't clear or easy. We dash away from the trail at times; we wander without knowing we've just entered enemy territory.

Heartache

However Samson got into there, he is willing to make himself right at home in the land of the Philistines. His parents try to talk him out of the marriage, which is forbidden by Mosaic Law. But they can't resist the demands of their strong-willed son.

Surely they wondered what would become of them and their Samson, whom they had dedicated to the Lord's service, to not only staying clear of Philistine influence but conquering their enemy. *Surely*, they must have anguished, *God isn't in this.*

But God is still at work (Judges 14:4). He is at work even when Samson first comes to Timnah, and he is at work when

Samson returns with his parents and finds himself in a vineyard.

Think about this picture. Not only has Samson returned to enemy territory, but he's dragged along his parents, and then left them to follow a road forbidden by not only Mosaic Law but his Nazirite vows. Samson is walking through the vineyard, surrounded by clutching vines and the heavy, sweet scent of grapes, and he has walked right into everything his life was dedicated to abstain from . . . and this is when a deafening roar stops him in his tracks.

Only Samson does not fall to the ground.

He whirls around to face a young lion leaping in attack, and with bare hands Samson tears it to death for "the Spirit of the LORD came upon him mightily" (v. 6 NASB). This is Samson's first experience of the supernatural strength that he has when God is with him.

"But he didn't tell his parents what he had done" (v. 6 MSG).

Don't you find this strange?

I think of my Christian, also an only child like Samson, and I cannot imagine for one moment how any male child who has just performed a feat of seemingly impossible brute strength would keep it to himself. If Christian squishes a bug, I hear about it—in gruesome detail.

Did Samson want to keep the knowledge of this incredible power to himself so that he could use it as he willed? Or was he wanting to keep from his parents the breaking of one more of the Nazirite vows by touching a dead body?

We are not told either way, but here is another point about what happens when you are asked to trust. Things aren't always explained to you. Some things simply are what they are, no reasons given, no meaning ascribed.

Mysteries and riddles don't mean God is absent, or not to be trusted.

Especially Samson shows us this. He enters enemy territory, drags his trusting parents into disobedience with him, pursues a marriage that breaks the core of his life's service and vows, breaks his remaining vows by walking through a vineyard; not only causes death but handles it—drips in it—by ripping apart a lion, and then plans a wedding day that should have been a war date.

And God is not only with the untrusting Samson, but comes upon him mightily.

The Big Day

Several weeks pass, and it is time for the wedding. Once more, Samson makes the trip back to Timnah. Once again, he makes a detour into the forbidden vineyard, this time to see what has become of the lion's carcass.

He is greeted by a strange sight. A swarm of bees has made itself at home in what is now the skeletal remains of the lion. The bees have been busy and produced honey inside the carcass. Samson scoops out some of the honey to eat, then collects more to give his parents—without telling them where he got it, since for a Nazirite, to eat anything from the carcass of a dead animal is an intentional flaunting of noncommitment to his vows.

Meanwhile, "his father went on down to make arrangements with the woman, while Samson prepared a feast there" (Judges 14:10 MSG). Now the "feast" here is a weeklong drinking party, and it seems unlikely that the groom doesn't join in with the festivities. In fact there is nothing in Samson's character to suggest he is the kind of man to deny himself anything he wants. So since Samson hasn't brought any groomsmen with him, the Philistines provide thirty men to be his companions. It's quite likely they are doing this not just to be friendly and welcoming, but to know what kind of man is this Samson, who is all too ready to trust his enemies.

The atmosphere is a little tense at first, so Samson decides to liven up things a bit with a riddle. He seems proud of his experience with the lion and the honey, even though it was a disobedient one, and now he becomes even more outrageous and makes a joke of it all:

Out of the eater came something to eat.
Out of the strong came something sweet. (Judges 14:14 ESV)

Samson tells the men that if, within the seven days of the feast, they can solve the riddle, he will give them each a linen outfit and a change of clothes. If they can't answer correctly, they have to give the same to him. This was an expensive bet, so after trying for three days to come up with an answer the men tell Samson's new wife to get the solution to the riddle or they will burn her father's house to the ground—with her in it.

With that incentive, she asks Samson to tell her the answer to his riddle. He refuses, having too much fun. For the next three days, she cries and complains and accuses Samson of not loving her; so on the seventh day he gives in and gives up to her the answer to the riddle. Never mind that their marriage, by custom, is to be consummated that night. Samson, trusting in his own ways, hasn't thought through or been too concerned about consequences before, and he's not thought of them now either.

When the Philistines tell him the solution to his riddle, Samson suddenly realizes that his new wife has betrayed him, for she was the only one he told. True to character, he flies into such a rage that he races into a town twenty miles away, kills thirty men with his bare hands, takes their clothes, and gives the winners of his bet their spoils.

In the meantime, Samson is so disgusted with his wife, that he's left his new home without consummating their marriage.

What Now?

Have you noticed where Samson's trust in himself gets him? Pretty much nowhere, but he is not willing to admit that. At this point in his life, Samson could have given in to trust God; he could have repented and God would have forgiven and restored him. God has been waiting for this all along, passionate to pour out mercy and restore him.

But once again Samson has plans of his own. As soon as his temper cools off, he decides to go and visit his wife.

Now the Hebrew word in Scripture used for "visit" is an Akkadian word, meaning that this is a culturally awkward marriage. (Do you think?) Instead of going to live with her new in-laws in another culture, Samson's bride remained with her family and her husband could "visit" her. So when Samson, with Philistine blood on his hands, shows up at his father-in-law's house, things are indeed—ahem—awkward. Samson announces that he has stopped by for his first conjugal visit, and he is told that it is too late.

> Her father wouldn't let him in. He said, "I concluded that by now you hated her with a passion, so I gave her to your best man. But her little sister is even more beautiful. Why not take her instead?" (Judges 15:1–2 MSG)

Samson is furious. He captures three hundred jackals (maybe not so superhuman since jackals travel in packs) and he ties them in pairs by their tails. Then he sets fire to the tails and sends the poor creatures into the Philistines' olive orchards and piles of standing grain.

All is consumed, including the Philistines, who are enraged. They want revenge. But afraid to tackle Samson directly, they take his wife and her father and murder them instead.

Now Samson, he is incensed. We don't know how many people he kills that day or what weapons he uses; but we are told his revenge is a great slaughter, and it sends Samson packing for the hills, where he hides in a cave.

Reflection

Have you noticed how violence always escalates? One side does something to put an end to it, and the other side comes back even stronger. It's the same in relationships. A harsh word is spoken, someone retaliates, the emotions build, and a gulf appears.

"A soft answer," the Scripture says, "turns away wrath, but a harsh word stirs up anger" (Proverbs 15:1).

Was Samson beginning to understand this? I wonder what he was thinking as he hid in that cave. He has a lot of blood on his hands, and his wife and father-in-law are now dead. He's set in motion a series of tragic events, and it's only about to get a lot worse.

When the rest of the Philistines hear what has happened in Timnah, a large company sets off to find Samson and execute him. They camp in Judah, and when the Israelites see this vast army of men, they are terrified. *Why*, they want to know, *have they come to fight now?*

They are told that the men are looking for Samson. The

Israelites tell the Philistines that they will bring in Samson.

How ironic that this is the only time in Samson's judgeship that the Israelites gather an army—and it is to capture him.

And that is how the Israelites find themselves gathering with three thousand men at the mouth of a cave to confront Samson. "Do you not know that the Philistines rule over us?" they ask him. "What is this you have done to us?" (Judges 15:11).

Samson has no desire to get in a fight with his own people, so he tells them that they can tie him up and deliver him to the Philistines as long as they promise not to harm him.

Samson's own people are afraid of him, so they bind him as tightly as they can with new ropes and lead him away to the Philistine camp.

What a sad picture of what happens when trust has been broken. Samson has been called to deliver his people from the domination of the Philistines, and instead here his people are delivering him to them.

An Amazing Victory

But even this God uses for the good, for the plan he is working. For as soon as the Philistine army can see Samson being brought to them, they charge toward him, shouting. And the Spirit of the Lord comes upon Samson again. He bursts the ropes as if they are made of fragile thread. Then he finds the jawbone of a donkey, still fresh enough to be pliable, and single-handedly kills one thousand men.

Not one of the Israelites picks up a weapon to help him; they just stand there in stunned amazement as their foolish judge, empowered by God, decimates the Philistine troops.

How amazing it is that God is still with Samson. Even though

Samson has broken God's trust, and two of his three vows, God has not left Samson.

Perhaps God saw in Samson's heart a feeble desire to protect the people he was called to serve. Perhaps God knew that deep down Samson wanted to spare the Israelites any further harm. After all the young, mighty Samson allowed himself to be bound, and he could easily have escaped from the cave, but must have known that meant leaving his people as easy prey.

Maybe there was some glimmer of trust flickering not just in the arrogant Samson's eye but deep within his heart. But is it too late? Is there a point where we go too far, repeat the same sin too often, and our trust in God evaporates, his love for us erodes?

Samson's life raises these questions for all those around him, if not himself. One too many times, it seems, he has played Russian (or Philistine!) roulette with his vows and got away with it. One of the only vows he hasn't broken is the one his mother was told, before his birth, by the angel from God . . . only that is about to change.

Delilah

Many of Samson's problems come from his lust for women, and it would be another woman who would lead to his downfall. He fell in love with a woman named Delilah. Those who were in charge of the Philistine armies were desperate to put an end to this man who had mocked them in so many ways, so they told Delilah that if she could discover the secret of his superhuman strength, they would pay her a great deal of money. Their desire was not to simply kill him—that would be too quick. They wanted to neutralize his power, capture, and torture him. They were humiliated that one man had been able to slaughter one thousand Philistine soldiers.

Samson has never been in more danger, not because of those

who are out to destroy him but because of his own broken, sinful nature. Unlike Joseph, who ran from a woman who was trying to trap him, Samson kept coming back for more. He still hasn't gotten it that no one could take away what God had given him. No, he would have to give it to them. And so he does.

For three nights in a row, soldiers hide in Delilah's bedroom as she tries to persuade Samson to reveal the secret of his strength. Each time he tells her something that isn't true. But on the fourth night, Samson commits the greatest sin of all: he reveals the source of his strength and anointing to an unbeliever.

Now the Philistine soldiers have left in frustration by this time, but when Samson tells Delilah about his hair, she knows it's the truth and summons back the soldiers.

She entices Samson to fall asleep on her lap, and you can almost imagine how she is stroking his brow, toying with his long locks. Samson slumbers in every way, spiritually and physically, and while he sleeps, his head is shaved.

Now it is Delilah's turn to have some fun. For the fourth night in a row, she wakes Samson: "The Philistines are upon you!"

Samson leaps up ready to fight—but it's all over.

What Scripture tells us here is one of the saddest things in God's Word: Samson "did not know that the LORD had left him" (Judges 16:20 NIV).

His strength is gone.

The soldiers grab him and gouge out his eyes. It's not enough for Samson to be broken, he must be blinded too, they decide, and then they put him to work on a large wheel in a prison, grinding grain like a beast of burden. For that is what Samson finally feels: that he is a beast, that his life is a burden.

Finally, unwilling to fall to his knees on his own, Samson is felled and trapped like an animal.

But he is still a child of God.

God's Secret

What the Philistines haven't reckoned with is the same thing that can trip up you and me: the fact that as long as you have one breath left in your body, it is not too late to start again. God's plan secures a way for us to come to him, and even Samson, stumbling blindly now in circles, begins to see this truth.

A curious thing happens too. As things become clearer to him, Samson's hair begins to grow again. Of course Samson's true power was never in his hair, but in God. Still, his hair is a symbol of his commitment, a consecration. So as he pushes that wheel day after day, closed into the darkness, being mocked and spat upon by those who pass him, Samson talks to his Father God, and he asks for one more chance to finally trust. To give God the glory.

The idea of trusting God, you see, has finally kicked in for Samson, and he longs to knock his enemies to their knees. Not just the Philistines, but also the enemies of isolation and separation, pride and lustful passion, despair and debauchery.

So the Philistines gather together to offer a sacrifice to their god, Dagon, whom they believe has delivered Samson into their hands. And what appears to be an ultimate humiliation for Samson begins to unfold as part of God's plan. For once the Philistines are drunk, they have Samson brought out of prison to entertain them.

The blinded Samson, led into the fray by a young man, asks for permission to rest on the pillars holding up the courtyard.

This place of his humiliation is his holy ground, for it is here that he appeals one last time. "O Lord GOD, remember me, I pray! Strengthen me, I pray, just this once, O God, that I may with one blow take vengeance on the Philistines for my two eyes" (Judges 16:28).

Samson has just asked God to let him die with the Philistines so he could do in his death what he had been unwilling to do in his life—and God, in his tender mercy, answers Samson's prayer. God gives Samson his strength back, and Samson, finally trusting with everything he has in his arms and back, his heart and soul, brings the house down on them all.

The Ultimate Trust

In his failure, all Samson could do was trust God. That was all he had ever had to do, but he got in the way.

We do that a lot too.

Making a very poor choice can be so easy, and playing with danger can be very appealing at times. You may be bored with your life and think, *What harm can a little adventure over to the darker side of who I am do?*

The trouble with first steps is that they inevitably lead to a second and a third. Wherever you stand at the moment is your holy ground, and grace is available there.

All it takes is trust in God.

For some people, trusting God in the environment in which they live is very costly. Even as I write, I have friends who are in prison because of their faith—everything they live and believe is an offense to the culture where they have been called. For others, an open profession of faith in Christ can cost a career or a promotion.

The question, then, is can you harbor a private trust in God—is it possible to be a secret disciple?

The two men we are about to meet wondered this very thing, and they sought their answers in the night.

ELEVEN

TRUSTING GOD WHEN YOU HAVE A LOT TO LOSE

The Beauty of Giving Your All

Here I stand; I can do no other. God help me. Amen!

—MARTIN LUTHER, SPEECH OF THE "DIET OF WORMS," APRIL 18, 1521

There was a man of the Pharisee sect, Nicodemus, a prominent
leader among the Jews. Late one night he visited Jesus and
said, "Rabbi, we all know you're a teacher straight from God.
No one could do all the God-pointing, God-revealing acts you
do if God weren't in on it."

—JOHN 3:1–2 MSG

S everal years ago, I had the honor of being part of a team of singers and speakers taking part in a very special weekend in Tallinn, Estonia—that tiny country in the Baltic region of northern Europe, bordered by Sweden, Finland, and Russia.

During World War II, Estonia was occupied and annexed by the Soviet Union and then by the Third Reich until 1944, when it was reoccupied by the Soviet Union. Estonia remained under Soviet Union rule until regaining its independence on August 20, 1991—the same autumn I was to take part there in the country's very first Christian concert and crusade. Ironically, the event was set to take place in the Communist Party headquarters.

So in August I flew from Los Angeles to Moscow, where I spent the night on the first leg of my journey. The next day I would head for Tallinn, Estonia.

Wandering around Moscow, everything seemed very gray, both the buildings and the people. No one made eye contact or exchanged simple pleasantries. The only person who spoke to me was a young Russian girl who wanted to buy my American jeans, but as I was wearing them at the time, that would have been difficult.

One of the more bizarre things available to Russian citizens and tourists alike is standing in line for hours to view the body of Russian revolutionary Vladimir Lenin, who died in 1924. Lenin wanted to be buried in his family plot, but Joseph Stalin insisted on putting his body on public display in Red Square. So Lenin's body lies in a glass case, watched by government scientists—a little like Snow White but not as cute.

Twice a week the case is dusted, and twice a year the body is removed and dipped in a blend of eleven herbs and chemicals.

Curious about it all, I stood in line for a while, but the line moved so slowly and the armed guards looked extremely disapproving. A friend who had traveled in Russia before had advised me that at the mausoleum I had to look suitably somber or I could be pulled out of line and fined. I wasn't sure I could pull that off after a three-hour wait, so I left and went back to the hotel for dinner.

The menu was in Russian so I ordered something that had a nice name, not having a clue what it was. When it arrived it looked a bit like beef but was very chewy and tough. Later, I discovered my meal was roasted bear, which I concluded had died of old age.

The following morning I caught a cab back to the Moscow airport to board my Aeroflot flight to Tallinn.

Now I have never experienced a flight before or since like that one on Aeroflot, which is the national airline of Russia. For a start, there was no restriction on what you could bring on board, so it was a free-for-all. The seats were arranged so that you were facing the people in front of you; the man facing me had a big black dog who continuously drooled on my suede boots. Beside me, a drunken soldier kept falling asleep on my shoulder. Some seats didn't have seat belts, but no one seemed to mind. (I think my fellow passengers had resigned themselves to not surviving anyway.) And when the attendants came around with drinks, they had a pitcher of orange squash and about four cups. Basically you had to drink up and give it back for the next row. I decided to pass on that—and the black bread, which I gave to the dog.

Aeroflot, indeed, I thought. *This airline would be better named Aeroflop.*

All these minor inconveniences of foreign travel disappeared into the distance, however, when the plane landed in Tallinn. A large group of believers was there to meet me at the gate, singing hymns, and bearing arms full of flowers. And this was merely a prelude to the wonderful time when we met up with the rest of the American and Estonian teams for prayer before our event the following evening.

Freedom!

I will never forget being in the company of these believers who prayed in a language I didn't understand but with an overwhelming passion I couldn't mistake. I wept as they cried out to God for the people of their country. This was a new beginning for them, a chance to publicly proclaim the freedom that is found in Jesus Christ alone.

I thought about this through the following day as we met for a sound check in the large arena of the former Communist Party headquarters. I sat on the edge of the stage, imagining what messages had been proclaimed from this platform in previous years and who would gather here this night.

By 7:00 p.m., the place was packed. I noticed that there were armed guards in long gray coats standing at the back of the arena. We were assured that they were only observing and there was nothing to fear.

At the end of the concert, a young American evangelist, through an interpreter, shared the message of freedom in Christ.

It was an unforgettable sight to watch so many young people respond to his call, come to the front of the stage, and pray to receive a copy of the Bible. For many of these Estonians this was the first Bible they had ever seen, let alone possess. I marveled at their display of trust, and the changes within them and without.

Then, as I headed out of the arena to my host's car, I realized that one of the guards was headed right toward me. For a moment I wondered what I had done to stir his attention. I braced myself as the guard stopped in front of me, looked me straight in the eyes, and said, "I believe . . . long time now, I believe."

With that, he turned and left as quickly as he had approached.

How long, I wondered, praying for him, *has he felt pressured to keep his faith a secret? How much does trust in God cost one here?*

A Personal Matter

I am acutely aware that not just in Estonia, but many places around the world it is very dangerous, even life-threatening, to be a follower of Christ. In fact, I am part of a prayer group interceding right now for a young British woman being held in a prison with appalling conditions simply because she shared her faith with another woman in a Muslim country. Some of her friends and family have been critical of her choices, saying that faith is a private matter and should be kept that way. But this young woman disagrees, has trusted God enough to be open about her faith, and it is costing her dearly.

Perhaps it was easier before the death and resurrection of Christ to keep your faith private. You could have been a devout Jew who observed dietary restrictions and held a deep, profound, but largely private faith.

After Jesus came to earth, however—ministering in miracles across the country, teaching God's Word with insight and authority, rising from the dead—everything changed. He turned the world inside out, and tore down fences where many people wanted to perch with one foot in one world and the other foot in another. He divided those who believed in him from anyone who did not. He demanded that response: either decide he is a crazy man or choose to believe that he is who he says he is—the Son of God, the Christ, *Messiah*. And believing that, trusting him, following him, obeying him?

That would change everything.

Choosing Who to Trust

I can sit here in my office in Frisco, Texas, and write about making radical choices. But what must it have been like for those who walked on this earth with Christ when he began to teach?

The people in Jesus' day who were waiting for the Messiah had very strong ideas of what he would look like. For some, these ideas were so clearly defined in their own minds that they missed him altogether. Others thought Jesus might be the one, but if they were wrong, it would cost them everything, and did they trust him enough to turn over *everything*?

This is the question asked by two men who each met Jesus just before he was crucified. Both these men, Nicodemus and Joseph of Arimathea, were members of the important Jewish council, the Sanhedrin; and each of them was wealthy. Each had to decide whether or not to believe Jesus was the Messiah, and their decisions could cost them what trusting Jesus costs any of us, even today: power, position, money, influence.

To understand their stories, we must first understand what the people at that time knew about the coming Messiah.

For starters, they knew the word *Messiah* meant "anointed one," the one anointed by God and empowered by God's Spirit to deliver his people and establish his kingdom. (The Greek counterpart is *Christos*, from which we get the word *Christ*.) In Jewish thought, then, the Messiah would be the king of the Jews, a political leader who would defeat their enemies and bring in a golden era of peace and prosperity.

In the Old Testament, the word *Messiah* is used more than thirty times to refer to kings anointed and chosen by God; and several Old Testament books prepared God's people for what the Messiah would do:

- *Introduce the new covenant.* "'Behold, the days are coming,' declares the LORD, 'when I will make a new covenant with the house of Israel and the house of Judah'" (Jeremiah 31:31 ESV).
- *Preach the gospel.* "The Spirit of the Lord GOD is upon me,

because the Lord has anointed me to bring good news to the poor; he has sent me to bind up the brokenhearted, to proclaim liberty to the captives, and the opening of the prison to those who are bound" (Isaiah 61:1–2 ESV).

· *Bring peace.* "For to us a child is born, to us a son is given; and the government shall be upon his shoulder, and his name shall be called Wonderful Counselor, Mighty God, Everlasting Father, Prince of Peace" (Isaiah 9:6 ESV).

· *Be a priest.* "And say to him, 'Thus says the Lord of hosts, "Behold, the man whose name is the Branch: for he shall branch out from his place, and he shall build the temple of the Lord. It is he who shall build the temple of the Lord and shall bear royal honor, and shall sit and rule on his throne"'" (Zechariah 6:12–13 ESV).

· *Bring in everlasting righteousness.* "Seventy weeks are decreed about your people and your holy city, to finish the transgression, to put an end to sin, and to atone for iniquity, to bring in everlasting righteousness, to seal both vision and prophet, and to anoint a most holy place" (Daniel 9:24 ESV).

So for those Jews and converts who had been under the boot of the Roman Empire for so long, the Messiah would finally make things right:

> He won't judge by appearances, won't decide on the basis of hearsay. He'll judge the needy by what is right, render decisions on earth's poor with justice. His words will bring everyone to awed attention. A mere breath from his lips will topple the wicked. Each morning he'll pull on sturdy work clothes and boots, and build righteousness and faithfulness in the land. (Isaiah 11:4–5 MSG)

To the Jews, this meant the Messiah was to be an earthly king, and there would be a newly restored earthly kingdom. Israel had been told that through David's descendants the Messiah's throne would have dominion over all the earth forever. *Once more*, thought men like Nicodemus and Joseph of Arimathea, *Israel will have her place on the earth and her enemies will be defeated*.

No wonder they did not immediately recognize Jesus.

Not until age thirty did Jesus begin his ministry, and then he was a curious figure. He preferred hillsides and the seashore for a pulpit more than the Tabernacle. He told stories and spoke in riddles, rather than teaching as the Pharisees by condemning sinners and casting stones. He seemed more like a poet than a preacher, full of anger, laughter, love. He wept, and partied, and hung out with outlaws, preferring to roam the desert, often seeming on the run. Was he a charlatan? Or a magician? How could you explain some of his "tricks," like raising Lazarus from the dead, for instance? He was a man of mystery; not like other kings, who won battles and killed enemies to lead his people into bringing home slaves and spoils.

So while some people immediately dropped everything they owned to follow Jesus, others, like Nicodemus in particular, had to think it all through; they had to learn not to trust their own ideas and listen to what this unusual man from Nazareth had to say.

Joseph of Arimathea

The four gospel writers introduce us to Joseph, each with his own take on him.

Matthew indicates Joseph of Arimathea was an unlikely disciple:

> Late in the afternoon a wealthy man from Arimathea, a disciple of Jesus, arrived. His name was Joseph. He went to Pilate and asked for Jesus' body. Pilate granted his request. Joseph took the body and wrapped it in clean linens, put it in his own tomb, a new

tomb only recently cut into the rock, and rolled a large stone across the entrance. Then he went off. (Matthew 27:57–60 MSG)

The fact that Joseph was wealthy is something that Matthew, once a tax collector, would have noticed right away, and indeed that fact is remarkable.

After all, Jesus had said it is easier for a camel to go through the eye of a needle than for a rich man to enter the kingdom of heaven (Matthew 19:24); and not many Jews became rich under Roman rule in honorable ways. Indeed, the wealthy were often in the pocket of the Roman government and happy to cheat their own people by extorting more tax money from them than they owed, then pocketing a percentage.

Joseph, however, was not that kind of man. He didn't use his wealth to isolate himself from danger. Instead, he used his wealth to do what Peter and the other disciples should have done: ask for the body of Jesus. He did what the rich young ruler in Christ's parable in Matthew 19:22 would not do: step out and put his own life in danger as a follower of Christ.

Luke gives us a slightly different picture of Joseph. He lets us know that Joseph was a good man but identifies him as part of the Sanhedrin, the council that had condemned Jesus to death. Luke separates Joseph from the rest of the council by saying that he was waiting for the kingdom of God (Luke 23:50–54), but was Joseph holding back all that he really believed? Was Joseph wrestling to trust the truth because of all he might lose? In an earlier chapter of his gospel, Luke tells us:

When it was morning, the religious leaders of the people and the high priests and scholars all got together and brought him before their High Council. They said, "Are you the Messiah?" He answered, "If I said yes, you wouldn't believe me. If I asked what you meant by your question, you wouldn't answer me. So here's what I have to say: From here on the Son of Man takes his place at God's right hand, the place of power." They all said, "So you admit your claim to be the Son of God?"

"You're the ones who keep saying it," he said.

But they had made up their minds, "Why do we need any more evidence? We've all heard him as good as say it himself." (Luke 22:66–71 MSG)

Joseph was in that gathering, as was Nicodemus. But there is no record of either of them, or anyone for that matter, dissenting in the council. The one action at the end of the meeting was Christ dragged before Pilate.

I wouldn't presume for a moment to understand what it was like to be there that night. The tension and hatred in the room must have been intense. Everything was at stake.

In his book *Becoming Children of God: John's Gospel and Radical Discipleship*, Wes Howard-Brook observes that anyone who proclaimed Jesus as Messiah would be expelled from the synagogue and would have needed to renounce their status as Pharisees.[1]

John's gospel speaks even more plainly, as if to say, *Let's tell it like it really is.* John writes: "Nevertheless even among the rulers many believed in Him, but because of the Pharisees they did not confess Him, lest they should be put out of the synagogue; for they loved the praise of men more than the praise of God" (John 12:42–43).

Add to all this the account of the gospel of Mark. While much like Matthew's and Luke's accounts in describing Joseph, Mark adds two words (15:42–47): "prominent" and "boldly" (NIV). Each word speaks to turning points in Joseph's discipleship and you'll see how as his story unfolds.

The fact that Joseph was not just any member of the Sanhedrin but one of prominence is significant. He would be one of those looked to for leadership.

So why didn't Joseph say anything the night Jesus was being accused of heresy? Was he afraid of being harmed himself by the enraged, reactionary Sanhedrin? Or was he secretly putting a last hope—his trust—in Pilate who just might refuse to execute Jesus?

Time to Take a Stand

Have you ever been in a place like that, where you know something is wrong but you pray someone else will speak up so you don't have to? The situation might be as ordinary as the bullying behavior of one child at a party. You know all the other mothers see it too, but you don't want to step out and say something because you know it will offend. Or maybe in your work, something is going on that you know is wrong, and others know it too, but they're not speaking up, so why should you?

Every day we are faced with choices like these: Will we speak up, or will we be silent? Will we trust God to control any situation, or do we think that not getting involved can keep things in control while at the same time not cost us anything either?

The gospel writers who witnessed Jesus' ministry, crucifixion, and resurrection show us a Joseph of Arimathea who might have taken the "keep silent and stay out of trouble" mentality.

But Mark's gospel, using the word *boldly* to describe Joseph, shows us another side too. You see, Mark tells us that Joseph went to claim the body of the murdered Jesus—and that meant the humiliating, horrifying task of going before Pilate. Remember, the last Jew to stand before Pilate now hung lifeless on a cross.

What caused Joseph to break his silence? Had he witnessed the crucifixion? Was he there when Jesus asked God to forgive his murderers? Did Joseph hear Jesus groan to God that his work was finished?

The Scriptures don't detail Joseph's story between the Sanhedrin events and those after Christ's death, but Mark makes note of something remarkable: As Jesus breathed his last breath, the centurion standing as his executioner announced, "Truly this Man was the Son of God" (15:39). And then Joseph goes to Pilate to claim Christ's body.

Do you see the unmistakable mercy here?

At the moment and place of Jesus' deepest pain and shame, he allows for a Roman executioner to proclaim trust at his feet, and a man who did not speak up when he could have now has the chance to take his life and reputation in his own hands and ask for the battered body of Christ.

That is one of the most powerful effects of Christ's life—how he shows us what is in us. You see, Jesus brings all that is good and bad, fearful and courageous, compromised and steady into the light. Then his grace allows us to change, to trust. He never reveals our flaws to shame us, but to redeem us.

Do you see the grace here? Do you see that no matter how often you fail, it is never too late to take your place at Jesus' side, never too late to trust him? Do you see that God's love for us shows up more powerfully in our failures than in any of our greatest successes?

The Companionship of Brokenness

And here is where we see Nicodemus and Joseph of Arimathea together, and John's gospel gives us two details that the other writers omit:

> So [Joseph] came and took the body of Jesus. And Nicodemus, who at first came to Jesus by night, also came, bringing a

mixture of myrrh and aloes, about a hundred pounds. Then
they took the body of Jesus, and bound it in strips of linen
with the spices, as the custom of the Jews is to bury. (John
19:38–42)

Do you remember the criticism Mary received when she
anointed Jesus' feet with one pound of pure nard (John 12:3–5)?
Here, Nicodemus brings one hundred pounds of spices to anoint
Jesus' body. Why such a huge amount? Did he feel guilty because
he was in the Sanhedrin and hadn't taken a stand when Jesus was
alive? Was he finally moved to give up his wealth along with the
position and power to help bury Jesus?

We don't know why, but the amount does indicate that neither Nicodemus nor Joseph expected Jesus to rise again. No, they
expected Jesus' body to be in the grave for a very long time.

Nicodemus

So what do we know, really, of Nicodemus? We can understand
him best by looking at where power lay in Rome in those days.

Most of the Roman aristocrats were landowners. They controlled the rest of the population through the military, tax
collectors, and those who were in the governor's pocket. The
centurion whose servant Jesus healed fell into the first group,
Matthew and Zacchaeus into the second, and Caiaphas and
Nicodemus into the final one.

Yes, Nicodemus was of the Jewish power-and-wealth elite,
and there was an understanding between his "type" in the
Sanhedrin and the Roman authorities: *You allow us our free-
doms, and we will make sure people stay in line, pay their taxes,
and don't even think of rebellion.*

But Nicodemus was curious about Jesus: *What if Jesus was the long-awaited Messiah?* So the young ruler comes to talk with Jesus at night, either out of fear of being seen or to make it clear that this is not an "official" visit. And, interestingly, Nicodemus calls Jesus "Rabbi," which shows that he is open to following the carpenter from Nazareth:

> There was a man of the Pharisee sect, Nicodemus, a prominent leader among the Jews. Late one night he visited Jesus and said, "Rabbi, we all know you're a teacher straight from God. No one could do all the God-pointing, God-revealing acts you do if God weren't in on it."
>
> Jesus said, "You're absolutely right. Take it from me: Unless a person is born from above, it's not possible to see what I'm pointing to—to God's kingdom." (John 3:1–3 MSG)

Jesus cuts right through the compliment to the issue at hand—life. He says, essentially, *This is your life we're talking about, Nicodemus, not debating or swapping religious ideas. Do you want to live forever?*

The exchange that follows is fascinating.

Nicodemus asks, "How can a man be born when he is old? Can he enter a second time into his mother's womb and be born?"

Jesus answers, "Most assuredly, I say to you, unless one is born of water and the Spirit, he cannot enter the kingdom of God" (John 3:4–5).

Water and Spirit

To be born of water and be born of Spirit, one is a public act, and the other takes place in private. Here Jesus makes clear that both births are public for anyone to follow him into the kingdom of God. Nicodemus cannot follow Christ secretly, for following Jesus must transform your world, turn everything inside-out and upside-down.

Nicodemus hears this idea and sadly leaves Jesus. He thinks about what this public, inside-out, upside-down business must mean.

Fast-forward now to the Feast of Tabernacles. This is one of the oldest and most joyous of Jewish feasts, a celebration of the end of harvest. Jesus stands up in the temple during the feast and says, "If anyone thirsts, let him come to Me and drink. He who believes in Me, as the Scripture has said, out of his heart will flow rivers of living water" (John 7:37–38).

The Pharisees seethe. Jesus, they believe, is taunting them. The Pharisees send a group of temple guards to arrest Jesus, but the guards return without him. When questioned, the guards say, in their defense, that they have never heard anyone speak like this before. This enrages the Pharisees who accuse the guards of being deceived by Jesus.

One of the guards makes an interesting comment: "Have any of the rulers or the Pharisees believed in Him?" (7:48). Although this is phrased like a question, it was purely rhetorical, the implied answer being, "Of course not!"

And Nicodemus is in the room. He must have been there when the Pharisees sent the guards to arrest Jesus, and said nothing. This time he speaks up. "Does our law judge a man," Nicodemus asks, "before it hears him and knows what he is doing?" (7:51).

Nicodemus hopes and prays that the Pharisees' love and reverence for the law will be enough to save Jesus, without having to speak more from his own heart. But as he discovers, reverence and law have nothing to do with justice for those who don't believe in or trust Jesus.

A Time to Stand Up

Now think of the crucifixion. Whether they were there to see it all, we don't know. But after Jesus gasps his last breath, Joseph is standing in the courtyard of the Roman ruler.

Pilate doesn't believe Joseph when he asks for Jesus' body because Jesus is dead.

Jesus is dead? Pilate is incredulous. *It's only been six hours. A healthy man can often writhe on the cross for two to three days.*

So at first Pilate will not entertain Joseph's request.

But Joseph is adamant and perhaps beginning to become frantic too. It's almost sunset before the Sabbath, and Jesus' body must be buried before the end of the day of his death, according to Jewish custom.

Pilate sends for the centurion to ask if this is true or if he's being tricked. *Perhaps,* he may have thought, *Jesus has slipped into a coma, and these Jews are attempting to steal the body and revive him.*

The centurion assures Pilate that Jesus is indeed dead.

Pilate releases the body to Joseph's care.

It was not an easy job to take the dead body of a grown man off a cross. Joseph unrolls a fresh white linen cloth on the ground, longer than the height of a man and twice as wide. This is the burial shroud in which Jesus will be wrapped. Then Joseph leans a ladder against the back of the cross and climbs to the top. Imagine his view from there, Jesus' blood-streaked face, the crown of thorns pressed into his brow.

Joseph attaches ropes around Jesus' chest and under his arms. Tossing the rope to the centurion to hold, Joseph would have to wrench the nail from the flesh of one wrist, then the other. As the soldier takes the weight of Christ's body, Joseph descends the ladder and pulls the last nail from Jesus' ankles.

Now the battered, broken body is stretched upon the fresh white linen.

Joseph and Nicodemus carry Jesus to the tomb and anoint his body with a king's ransom in myrrh and aloe. Can you imagine how they may have lingered, what they must have been thinking? *Thirty-three years old. Now gone. We will never see him again. We will never hear more of his stories. He will never explain to us more of the Scriptures. Why couldn't we save him?*

Finally, they must go. Leaving Jesus may be the hardest part of all this, the part they didn't know could hurt so much. Regretfully, they leave the tomb and heave a stone across its entrance.

And this is the last we read in the New Testament about Nicodemus.

The Beginnings of Trust

Christian tradition tells us that Nicodemus is baptized by Peter and John, persecuted by hostile Jewish forces, and loses his place on the Sanhedrin.[2]

How did the rest of Nicodemus's life turn out? Did he do as Jesus asked and leave everything? That would have meant losing his place of power and position. But was that really a loss, considering Jesus then saved his life? Nicodemus heard and saw directly from Jesus what it meant to be born again and to live and trust God in public and in private.

And what of Joseph of Arimathea? The *Bible Exposition Commentary* describes him as "God's secret agent in the Sanhedrin."

Beyond that we know few details of his outcome.

I wonder, though, where was Joseph when he heard the news that the tomb he'd given for Jesus was available again? Did he finally believe, finally trust, that Jesus was the resurrected Son of God? Or had Joseph already believed this a long time, and just never been able to wrest away his fears to trust Christ and proclaim him?

I wonder, since it seems strange that Joseph had a tomb so close to the site of Jesus' execution. Most pious Jews wanted to be buried in the Holy City, and a rich man like Joseph could have afforded a prime location away from the cries of dying criminals. Perhaps God spoke to this man and told him to make a tomb ready, just as God had told Noah to build a boat; maybe Joseph, like Noah, obeyed the voice of God that he heard. Maybe Joseph was put on the earth to serve "for such a time as this," and certainly he gave lavishly to care for the body of the murdered Jesus.

How beautiful is that kind of trust from God: to allow one, even a doubting, fearful one, to hold the broken Christ, the Christ broken for you and me, in his hands.

The mercy and grace of God, you see, shines through the broken places of those then and now who fall and rise up again. That is the mystery and majesty of our Lord, that even if you show up a little late, his welcome is the same.

You may have some regret for those years when trusting God seemed too risky. What would it cost? What would it mean for your family? What would God ask you to do?

It is never too late to step out and trust. You are invited to get back on that swing and feel how beautiful it is to fly high in the arms of God.

Nicodemus and Joseph had to leave behind everything they knew to start again in a new city, but they were starting with the experience of having seen Jesus with their own eyes and knowing him as the risen Son of God. What if you were called to follow God, too, leaving behind everything you have—but the call was your first introduction to the truth that God is real and personal? Would you start to trust him when you have no history with him?

That would be quite a journey, and I know one who could describe it.

TWELVE

Trusting God with Your Journey

The Beauty of a Pilgrim

If we try to resist loss and change or to hold on to blessings and joy belonging to a past which must drop away from us, we postpone all the new blessings awaiting us on a higher level and find ourselves left in a barren, bleak winter of sorrow and loneliness.

—Hannah Hurnard

God told Abram: "Leave your country, your family, and your father's home for a land that I will show you."

—Genesis 12:1 msg

Barry, Christian, and I loved our life in Nashville. We lived in a home that backed up to the golf course, which almost guaranteed I would get to see my sister every summer. Her husband, Ian, you see, is an avid golfer, and as they are both teachers, they have long summer vacations—perfect for flying over from Scotland to see their wee sister!

So Nashville afforded us a wonderful gathering place for family, and Christian was in a good school there and doing well. We felt pretty settled, apart from two issues that raised their heads every now and then.

The first was that all the women I work with on the Women of Faith team live in Frisco, Texas, a few miles north of Dallas—and they have become family for Barry, Christian, and me. This is because, as the Women of Faith team, we are a pretty tight-knit community on the road. Plus Barry is an only child whose mom and dad both died within the past few years, and all my family still lives in the United Kingdom. So we crave our together time, but it's difficult living so far apart.

That was the other issue: travel. When you fly thirty weekends a year, it is very helpful to live close to an airline hub. Dallas is a hub for American Airlines, so almost every city that we travel to is just one flight from Dallas but two flights from Nashville. When you are really tired after a wonderful but exhausting weekend, it's hard to fly to Dallas and wait for that connection to Nashville.

Could We Have a Sign, Lord?

Every time Barry and I talked about the possibility of moving to Frisco we had two major issues: we needed to sell our house, and we wanted to get Christian into a good school. We prayed about it, talked to our closest friends, and felt like it could be a good thing.

So we put our house on the market and began to make inquiries about schools in Texas.

One of our dearest friends, Ney Bailey, who lives in Frisco, told us about a school she had heard great things about; I went to the school's website and liked what I saw. Another friend, Josh McDowell, recommended the school highly, so I called and talked with a very helpful woman in admissions. Christian would be going into second grade, and she said that there were still three places available. I asked her to send any paperwork necessary, but we still had a house to sell.

Quite a few people looked at our house, but there were no offers. As the weeks passed, it began to seem clear that God was closing the door on this move. The school had given me a final cutoff date in May, and even at that they were stretching for us; but the date came and there was no sign of a sale. I called the school and thanked the admissions counselor for her patience and grace. We agreed that perhaps next year God might open a door. We decided just to leave the house on the market as we wanted to scale down a bit anyway.

Then in June we had a nibble on the house—and it sold. Just out of curiosity I checked with the school in Texas to see if all three places had been filled, and they had. So we moved into an apartment in Nashville until we decided which side of town to look for a new home. Barry and I knew that as Christian got older, it would be important to live close to some of his friends and not too far away from school, especially since he loves sports. All sorts of driving to and from games was definitely in our future wherever we lived.

Abraham Didn't Have a Second Grader!

So life went on and soon it was the first week in July. Barry, Christian, and I were in Dallas on business. Barry had some

meetings, and I was working on a book deadline (a hobby of mine!).
Barry took Christian with him, and I was in a favorite coffee shop
to read my devotional for the day before I started writing.

The text was, "GOD told Abram [later called Abraham]: "Leave
your country, your family, and your father's home for a land that I
will show you" (Genesis 12:1 MSG).

As I read that verse, I had an overwhelming conviction that
God was saying, *Uproot and come to Dallas*, but it made no sense to
me at all.

I prayed, "Abram didn't have a second grader, Lord, so it was
easier for him to uproot his camels and his donkeys and pitch his
tent somewhere new. He didn't even have to sell his house—he
just took it with him."

The conviction wouldn't lift.

"Lord, you know that all I want to do is follow you, but there
are no places left in the school for this year."

At that very moment my cell phone rang. It was a Texas area
code, so I thought Barry was calling me from the Women of Faith
offices. Only when I answered, it wasn't Barry on the line—it
was the school counselor at the Texas school we'd checked out.
She said one place had just opened up in second grade—did we
want it?

My heart fluttered. How long, I asked, did we have to decide?
She told us she could only give us until five o'clock that evening.
I left my computer and coffee on the table and walked outside.

"What should we do, Lord?"

Go!

Are You Sitting Down?

I called Barry and asked him if he was sitting down, which he
immediately did. He detected something in the tone of my voice

that might indicate such a position would be helpful. I told him about my devotional and the phone call I had just received and asked him what he thought.

"What do you think?" he asked.

"I think we should go," I said, "but I want us to be in agreement on this—it's a big deal."

"Honestly," he said, "I don't have strong feelings one way or the other, so if you do, I think we should trust that."

"All right, then, do you think you could buy a house today?" I asked.

Good thing he was sitting down. "You're kidding," he said, "right?"

"No, not at all, just take Mary and Ney and Luci with you. If you and Christian love it and they love it, I'll love it," I said. "I don't care what kind of house it is, just who's in the house."

Then I called the school and accepted the place for Christian while he and his dad drove around looking at houses. They, in the meantime, found one they liked, and it passed muster with my friends. The Realtor e-mailed me some photos, and it looked great to me, so we bought it.

The move happened even faster. It was easy to pack, since much of our stuff was in storage already. So in four weeks, after the movers loaded all our stuff into their truck, we drove to the airport to fly to Dallas. In just three days, Christian would start classes at his new school and our family would be new residents of Dallas!

I Never Knew My Dog Could Fly

The move still seems surreal, and there is one memory that will live with me forever. We only had one dog at the time, our

Bichon, Belle. I took her to the vet to get a certificate to say that she was cleared to fly. She had never been on a plane before, so I wasn't sure how she would do. The vet suggested that we might give her a small dog tranquilizer. I asked how dogs do with that, and was assured that less than one percent have an adverse reaction.

"What," I asked, "would an adverse reaction look like?"

"Well," the vet said, "instead of calming your dog, the medicine can cause her to become very boisterous."

Of course you have guessed by now that our darling Belle is the prize-winning champion in that one percent category. At first she was just going nuts in her little carry-on under my seat. I tried singing softly to her, but that just seemed to annoy her. People were starting to stare disapprovingly at us, so Barry suggested I take her out of her carrier and hold her. Just at that moment Christian decided he needed to go to the bathroom so I handed Belle to Barry and walked with Christian to the rest room at the front of the plane.

I was waiting outside the door for Christian when I became aware of a strange noise. I looked back at our seats and Belle was flying! Barry had her by the back legs and she was flinging herself in the air like she was Super Bichon.

I was no help at all. I laughed so hard that I ended up on the floor of the cabin! Back in our seats, we all tried to calm Belle and finally made it safely to Dallas to settle in for the next part of the adventure.

The Call

Have you ever had an experience like that? Not the flying dog part, but a *knowing* that God was asking you to let go of what was familiar and move on to a new place or situation that requires, if not a leap of faith, at least a little jump in trust? There are so many questions involved:

- Is God telling me to do this, or am I just imagining that because of my own wants?
- What if I get this wrong?
- If I miss God, will I have blown his plan for my life?
- If it is God speaking here and I don't follow what I hear, will I miss his best for me?

The Bible is full of stories of men and women who got it right and got it wrong, some who stepped out in trust and others who trusted their own will instead—and through all their stories is a common thread—the faithful love of God.

Of all these stories, there is none quite like Abraham's (I'll refer to him as *Abraham* because it gets a little messy going back and forth between *Abram* and *Abraham*). Even though he is called the "father of faith," he didn't start out with a great amount of faith. He struggled with the urge to trust his own self, made mistakes, and almost ruined God's plan for his life on more than one occasion. Still, God remained faithful to direct his steps.

A Pattern to Follow

So many people think the moment God told Abraham to "go," and Abraham did, is the remarkable beginning of Abraham's journey in trust. But Scripture shows us God was preparing Abraham for that moment and that journey long before Abraham even heard God's call:

Terah took his son Abram, his grandson Lot (Haran's son), and Sarai his daughter-in-law (his son Abram's wife) and set

out with them from Ur of the Chaldees for the land of Canaan.
But when they got as far as Haran, they settled down there.
(Genesis 11:31 MSG)

You see, Abraham's father, Terah, began the process of
moving to the Promised Land, but stopped short of Canaan and
settled in Haran. This was a time in history where there were
great population shifts in the Middle East; it would not have
been unusual to see large families with their servants and live-
stock traveling across the desert. So when God appeared to
Abraham and told him to leave the place where he was, and go
to a place that would be revealed, Abraham was somewhat
familiar with what that looked like. His father had already mod-
eled it for him.

The fact that God chose Abraham for such a journey was not
a random choice either, but all part of the redemptive plan that
God promised generations ago, beginning with Adam and Eve in
the garden of Eden.

Even when the first man and woman decide not to trust and
obey God, you see, God still makes a way back to him. He gives
Adam and Eve children, and their direct descendant, the tenth
patriarch in line from Adam, is Noah. Now in Noah's day, only
he was trusting and obeying God. All the rest of humanity had
become so corrupt in such a short period of time that God wiped
the earth clean with a flood. You know the rest of that story:
Noah and his family, being righteous by trusting God, are the
only people saved—because God has a plan; because Noah's son
Shem will have children and grandchildren and great grandchildren and great, great grandchildren. (You get the idea.)
And that tenth patriarch in line from Shem is Abraham. And
God promises Abraham not once but on three separate occasions (Genesis 13:16; 15:5; and 15:15) a full life, a peaceful

death, a long legacy, and descendants as many as the sands in the desert and the stars in the sky.

Trusting God Has a Way for You

It's amazing this plan that God has for Abraham, from the very beginning of his journey in Genesis 12, and along the way, and even after some missteps by Abraham and doubts by Sarah. Both Abraham and Sarah must have wondered if they were crazy—or God was—because by the time God promises Abraham to "make him a great nation" Sarah is already an old woman—and they are childless.

Remember how devastating it was in those times for a woman to be barren? Everyone around Abraham and Sarah must have seen her barrenness as a sign of God's displeasure; they would have been tempted to believe that.

That, I think, is the whole point. We don't always see it, are tempted not to trust it, but the fact remains God is always making a way for you that's according to his grand plan.

Think about it: Sarah is barren and old, so it would be crystal clear to everyone that this child was from God. This gift was a direct intervention, no mistake.

Have you ever found yourself in that place in your journey where you have lost heart? You have waited patiently for what you believe God has promised you, and now it seems humanly impossible. That's the point for you and me, too, because it's there, exactly in these kinds of circumstances, where God does some of his best work.

Moses, another great patriarch, shows this. After he killed the Egyptian who was abusing a slave, he ran away and spent forty years working with sheep. Forty years is a long time. If that were to happen to me today, that would put me at ninety-two! (By the way, doesn't it seem to be the perfect training ground for Moses? Forty years with dumb, stubborn sheep and then forty more with the children of Israel! I think I'd take the sheep.)

If anything, the lives of Moses, Abraham, and Sarah are testaments to the fact that living in trust is in all the everyday things as well as in our big, life dreams.

You can know this today as you walk through the mall or sit in the carpool lane. Maybe you think you are fooling yourself to believe—to trust!—that God has a special plan for you. Just remember that even a casual observer could have looked at Abraham and his family as they made their way to Canaan and thought, *They don't look so different from any other travelers*. We tend to see in our mind's eye this one group of people heading across the desert as if led by an angel, but there would have been lots of travelers coming and going. What separated Abraham and his family was the call of God on their lives that they heard and answered by following in trust.

Following, of course, means walking an often thorny path. God does not explain the reason for the pain. He didn't to Sarah, nor to Abraham. But just as he did for them, he gives us a promise and a purpose, and he maps it out so intricately, so perfectly, that we don't always see the way of it. He asks only for us to trust, to know with wonder that every grain of sand in the desert and star sprinkled into the night sky is there by his hand and his heart—and on purpose.

Nothing Is for Nothing

You'll be tempted again and again in this life not to believe that. Recently I turned on the television news to hear a voice say, "It all seems so pointless."

The coverage recounted violent storms that had ripped

through a small town in Oklahoma. "All these tears, all this pain, for what? Nothing!"

My heart ached for the elderly lady being interviewed as she stood in front of her decimated home. Although I certainly understood her pain and frustration, I thought again that for those who love God, nothing is for nothing. Our God is a redeemer, and there is not one tear that has ever fallen from your eyes that is lost to your Father. We are told in the book of Revelation, "The Lamb on the Throne will shepherd them, will lead them to spring waters of Life. And God will wipe every last tear from their eyes" (7:17 MSG).

What an awesome promise that God himself will reach down and wipe away any remaining tears on your face.

You may well ask, "But what about now? Where are my answers now? Why doesn't God move now? What do I do when I am twenty years into being stuck in the field with the sheep?"

You cling to the promises of God. That's what Abraham had to do. Think about what that looked like for him. God told him to get his family together and move from where they had settled and go . . . somewhere else. Abraham had lived in Ur for most of his life and then his father moved them to Haran. Both those cities were well established in Mesopotamia. They were the New York and LA of their day. But God said go—and so they left.

A Good Beginning

So Abraham has done what God asked and moved his family mile after mile into the land of Canaan and south to the Negev. At each place along the way, God shows him: *This will be yours and your descendants'*. So at each place Abraham stops and builds an altar as a symbol of God's promise.

Then Abraham hits his first hurdle: there is a famine in the land. Rather than ask God to provide as they remain in the place of promise, Abraham decides to take his family to Egypt. Almost every time Egypt is mentioned in the Old Testament, it is a place of human failure and self-reliance—a symbol of that place where trust in self and not in God leads to trouble, despair, a "lostness."

So it is for Abraham with this decision. He is putting God's redemptive plan in jeopardy. He is taking his family away from the place that God has told him to go, and he tells Sarah (then called Sarai), who is breathtakingly beautiful, to lie, to pretend that she is his sister.

So as soon as they arrive in Egypt, word gets to Pharaoh that there is a beautiful new woman in town. Of course he orders her to be brought to him and she is added to his harem.

What could Abraham have been thinking? What about the child of promise now?

This Isn't Working

There is always the temptation waiting for us around any corner to help out God a bit. This, for example, can happen: You believe that God has promised you a godly husband, but you're getting older and the guy you work with really likes you. So you rationalize, *Okay, he's not a believer, but he is a good guy. Perhaps he'll come to the Lord through my example*. And even though you know it could erode and eventually bring down your faith, you seriously think about marriage with this guy.

I was listening to the *New Life Live* radio program the other day and one caller described that very scenario. He called it "evangelistic dating." The only problem was that the girl he was seeing still was not a believer, and she was now pregnant.

Compromised trust and obedience always lead to trouble and consequences.

Abraham is about to discover this, and something about God's grace in our messes too.

In Egypt, Abraham is quite happy. Because he is the "brother" of one of Pharaoh's favorite new women, he is given all sorts of stuff. Isn't it amazing how stuff is usually what we are given to keep us quiet when we have compromised? Thank God that he loves us in spite of our pathetic sinful appetites.

So God strikes Pharaoh and his whole household with a mysterious illness, and the truth surfaces that Sarai is in fact Abraham's wife. They are allowed to keep all the wealth Abraham has accumulated, but they are kicked out of Egypt.

Can you imagine how humiliating this must have been?

I remember once sitting in a very nice restaurant in Los Angeles having dinner with a friend, when a woman came charging in and stopped at the table of a couple in front of ours. The woman who stormed in turned to the woman seated and said, "Do you think I'm stupid enough not to recognize that *bleep bleep* cheap cologne you wear? Leave my husband alone!" With that she threw a glass of water at her husband and told him that they were leaving—now.

He got up and meekly followed her outside. The other woman sat for a while before she was presented with what I imagine was a fairly large bill. I don't know if she was embarrassed or not, but I could have crawled under the table for her.

I wonder if Abraham felt a bit like that as he gathered up his family and hightailed it out of Egypt to retrace his steps back to Canaan.

That is always the way of wisdom, though, when we fall down: to make our way back to where we know we are right with God. Failure can push us further from home, or it can cause us to come running back into his arms, where he always waits to welcome us home.

A New Day

One of the hallmarks of Abraham's life is that every time he makes a mistake and is rescued by the mercy of God, he is a different man. His faith in the goodness and sovereignty of God grows exponentially.

By the time he leaves Egypt, Abraham is a very wealthy man, as is Lot, but the land they are on cannot support them both. So they decide to part ways.

Abraham allows Lot to choose first.

Some people over the years have criticized that decision, as if once more Abraham is jeopardizing the land God has promised him.

I don't read Genesis 13 that way. I believe that Abraham once more is establishing his feet on the rock of trusting God with his future, so he lets Lot choose. I see Abraham learning that his own failures are teaching him most about how trustworthy God is.

There's a beautiful lesson of trust here because one of the greatest challenges of trusting is our fear of messing up. We forget, or maybe never understood to begin with, that God doesn't ask us to get everything right. Rather, he asks us to step out and trust him with everything we have and are—as a beautiful gift to him.

Lot misses this:

> Lot looked. He saw the whole plain of the Jordan spread out, well watered (this was before GOD destroyed Sodom and Gomorrah), like GOD's garden, like Egypt, and stretching all the way to Zoar. Lot took the whole plain of the Jordan. (Genesis 13:10–11 MSG)

Here again there is an allusion to trust: Egypt is a land rich and well watered—it looks good. It's something you can see as lovely. How often do we choose, like Lot, by what we can see, what we deem beautiful, lush, and good?

So Lot chooses Egypt and settles initially close to Sodom, right on the edge of the Promised Land. But by chapter 14, he now lives in Sodom. He doesn't seem bothered at all that he has chosen to live outside the land that God has promised to Abraham, the land that would be blessed by God, or that the people of Sodom were flagrant in their disregard for God and his ways. Lot chooses to step outside of God's blessing and protection and is about to taste what that harsh reality feels like.

Genesis 14 opens with the story of a classic military battle between rival nations, one of which is Sodom. In the midst of the mayhem, Lot is kidnapped and carried off. When Abraham hears what has happened to his nephew, he gathers all his servants, all 318 of them, and sets off to the rescue. Now remember Abraham is not a young man here. He is heading for eighty years of age. But he is ready to do battle, putting his personal safety aside for the love and loyalty of his family. So he splits his men into groups and they attack at night; Lot is recovered and all the wealth that has been stolen from Sodom. But this is not without a cost. Abraham has made powerful enemies, including one of the kings behind the raid—Amraphel, king of Babylon.

Trusting Beyond the Borders

We tend to think that the Old Testament is all about the law and the New Testament about grace, but grace is everywhere in the Old Testament as well as the New because Jesus is there too.

In the Old Testament, Abraham can be seen as a type of Christ figure, a foreshadowing of the One who abandons all personal safety to fight for us.

After his battle for Lot, Abraham gets a glimpse into the depth of the love of God for his people. First, though, he is discouraged. He is a rich man in many ways, but he has no heir to pass on his inheritance. As things stood, all his wealth would pass on to the steward of his house, Eliezer of Damascus. Eliezer is a loved and trusted servant, but he is not Abraham's son.

Abraham, showing how we live out trust, talks to God about this heartache. He questions all the promises he's had from God along this journey about an heir and descendants, and a legacy.

God hears Abraham. He knows this isn't the first time Abraham must have wondered how all this would transpire. God assures Abraham that his heir will be a child from his own body:

> Then he took him outside and said, "Look at the sky. Count the stars. Can you do it? Count your descendants! You're going to have a big family, Abram!" And he believed! Believed GOD!
> (Genesis 15:5–6 MSG)

The form of the Hebrew verb used here for "believed" does not mean a one-time thing—it means an ongoing action. Abraham's trust, his ongoing faith, is blessing God. At almost one hundred years old, Abraham is taking God at his word. He asks God for a sign of this promise of his descendants, not because he doubts, but as a token of his faith; God, bursting with love, answers in a dazzling way:

> GOD said, "Bring me a heifer, a goat, and a ram, each three years old, and a dove and a young pigeon."
> He [Abram] brought all these animals to him, split them down the middle, and laid the halves opposite each other.
> (Genesis 15:9–10 MSG)

Was God planning a barbecue? No, he was preparing a covenant.

In those days, a covenant was a common form of agreement and there were basically two types—one between a powerful nation and a weaker nation, and the other between a king and a loyal subject who would be granted some land for his personal devotion. In either instance, there was never any question as to who was in control in these covenants. If a weaker nation tried to breach its covenant, it would be annihilated, as would a subject who removed himself from the protection of his king. Once the parties agreed to the covenant, both sides would then walk between the pieces of an animal cut in two. This was a visual picture of a physical reality, a way of saying, *If you breach this covenant, may you be torn in two like these animals.*

Amazing Grace!

So Abraham gathers all the animals God requires, slaughters them, and carves them in half, carefully laying each half on the side of a path that he expects to walk through according to custom. Birds of prey, smelling the fresh meat, circle overhead. Soon they are diving onto the carcasses. Abraham shoos them away. He must have determined, if not worried for a moment there, that the birds of prey would mess with all he's prepared for God. He must have been thinking: *Everything has to be just right.*

Who knows how long he chases at the vultures that would rob him of getting this just right. Who knows how hard he bats at them to leave alone all he's so carefully laid ready, but the sun is beginning to set and he's suddenly tired.

Abraham falls into a deep sleep and "terror and great darkness fell upon him" (Genesis 15:12 NASB).

This terror, God explains in a vision, is what it is like to live outside of trust with him; it is a lesser, lonely, and dark place. It is a place of slavery that God knows his people will choose, just like Lot choosing Egypt. It is a place where his people will go, and then be freed from, but then return to again and again—a place of loneliness, separated from the goodness of God, a place of imprisonment to self.

So God prepares a way for the people, long before they even know it or are a gleam in their parents' eyes. And then, in the darkness, the deep of night, instead of Abraham walking between the torn animals, God and only God goes through. He passes between the animals in the form of a smoking firepot and a flaming torch. The night is illuminated by God the living torch. And the terror, the loneliness apart from him, the imprisonment to self? It all goes up in smoke.

The Friend of God

Do you see how amazing this is? Iain M. Duguid in his book, *Living in the Gap Between Promise and Reality*, explains, "The one who would give the law was here showing that grace comes first, for this was a totally one-sided covenant. It depended entirely on God for its fulfillment. God, the ever-living One was saying, 'I would rather be torn apart than see my relationship with humanity be broken, the relationship that I have promised to establish through Abraham's descendants.'"[1]

Every other covenant known to man was based on two parties living up to an agreement, but God essentially says to Abraham—and to you and to me: *I alone will make this vow. You will mess up and fail, but I will never, never leave you! You will fall and rise up and fall again, but I will love you, and I am making a way for your redemption.*

Nothing in relationship with God depends on us getting it all right. His covenant takes care of that. We just get to love, trust, and follow him all the way home—and that's worth reminding yourself. Write it down somewhere; put it on a card and carry it with you until it's as familiar as the air you breathe.

Abraham, witnessing God's glory in the night, must have written this on his heart.

So he waits and keeps trusting and obeying. For years.

He has waited for such a long time for his own baby that maybe he doesn't see so clearly as he did when he was younger. Maybe it takes his vision a minute to focus. For one hot afternoon, as he sits at the entrance to his tent, he sees three figures approach through the shimmering heat. He immediately makes his visitors welcome and offers them the finest he has to eat and drink. But he doesn't realize that he is entertaining two angels on their way to judge Sodom—or that the other guest is Christ, the Lord himself.

The moment is significant. It is the only recorded instance in the Old Testament where the Lord sits and shares a meal with a man or woman—and he does this in friendship. In Scripture, David, the shepherd turned king, is said to have a heart after God (1 Samuel 13:14; Acts 13:22), but only Abraham is called God's friend (2 Chronicles 20:7).

Now Christ tells his friend Abraham that he will return to this area in about a year and Sarah will have a son.

Sarah. overhearing the conversation, laughs to herself.

The Lord hears her and asks why she is laughing.

At first Sarah denies her actions because, Scripture says, she is afraid (Genesis 18:15). I wonder, in part, if it's maybe because after all these years, the promise of a baby sounds too good to be true too.

No matter. Christ knows how hard we find it to trust, how wavering our hearts can be, how uncertain we become when we can't see for ourselves the intricacies of his grand plan. He knows and must wait excitedly for our vision to clear and focus. We see only the desert, only the night sky. But there is so much sand. There are so many stars. "But you did laugh," he tells Sarah (Genesis 18:15).

What he was also saying was, *Trust me.*

Trusting God All the Way Home

Trust is a hard word for some of us these days. Surveys tell us that at ever increasing rates we don't trust our political leaders or the banking system. We have lost trust in many religious leaders. Too many people lose trust in spouses or friends.

God, Abraham learned, is the one friend you can always, completely, 100 percent trust. You can trust God with everything you have and are, because he never has and never will fail you. And you would think Abraham knew that lesson well after crossing so much desert. But God's friend had one more mountain to climb—to show us, crystal clear, what trusting in God looks like. That mountain was in Moriah, and God asked Abraham to take there the son he waited on for so long. That's right, Isaac was finally born to Abraham when he was one hundred years old.

And when God called, Abraham said, "Here I am."

And God said:

"Take now your son, your only son Isaac, whom you love, and go to the land of Moriah, and offer him there as a burnt offering on one of the mountains of which I shall tell you."

So Abraham rose early in the morning and saddled his donkey, and took two of his young men with him, and Isaac his son; and he split the wood for the burnt offering, and arose and went to the place of which God had told him. Then on the third day Abraham lifted his eyes and saw the place afar off. And Abraham said to his young men, "Stay here with the donkey; the lad and I will go yonder and worship, and we will come back to you." (Genesis 22:2–5)

Notice two significant things about this passage:

1. *Abraham rose early*. Not only did Abraham obey, but he was eager to obey.
2. *Abraham said, "We will come back to you."* By this point in his relationship with God, Abraham knew that even if he had to stick a dagger in his own son's heart, God would bring him back from the dead because Isaac was the son of God's promise, and God never breaks a promise. There was not a second's doubt that they would both come back.

So Abraham makes the journey, and he makes offerings to God along the way, and Isaac and the two young servants with them must have thought this was a grand trip into the mountains.

On the third day of their journey, God tells Abraham where he wants the sacrifice and Abraham tells the servants to stay where they are—that he and Isaac are going to burn a sacrifice to God and worship him.

And so father and son grab wood for the sacrificial fire and begin to climb.

The mountain Abraham climbs that day is the most difficult one of his life. It is the mountain of fear and doubt, the incline of *what ifs* and *what fors*. It is the mountain of *why* that he must crest to a summit of trust.

And he gets there, putting one step in front of the other, trusting, thinking how on the mountaintop he is closer to those stars God showed him many years ago.

At the top he prepares the sacrifice to worship God, and Isaac helps and wonders aloud where the animal is. And Scripture doesn't tell us if Abraham replies or weeps or what he is thinking.

We are told only what he does, and he is obeying. He has raised one hand with the knife to slaughter the sacrifice; in the other, he holds the fire to let the very promise he's loved the most burn and go up in smoke for the Lord.

It is only then, when Abraham's hand is ready to slay his only son, that God, who knows every emotion and heartache and hurt that his friend is feeling, shows up.

"Abraham," he calls, as an angel he has sent stills his friend's hand.

"Here I am!" Abraham answers, like God doesn't know. Moments of utter heartache, grief, and loss can cloud your thinking like that.

"Stop!" God says.

Abraham raises his eyes and there, caught in a bush by its horns, is a ram.

God has provided a ram to be sacrificed instead of Isaac!

It is not the last lamb that God will send.

There will be another Lamb, on another day, atop another mountain. How much God wishes to call "friend" all those for whom he delivers the sacrifice.

I don't know where you are in your journey of faith. You may just be starting out and wonder what lies ahead. You may have already crossed deserts, been waylaid in your own Egypt, or found yourself in that glorious place where you know that God is your faithful friend and can be trusted. Wherever you are, you are loved and there is even more grace for the days ahead. There are so many grains of sand, so many stars.

In any of these places, you can carry Abraham's story with

you. Like Abraham, you can move from one place to another, you can find resting spots, you will find ways out of dark places and have chances to be a new woman walking in the light—even if just by the light of the stars at night—moving ahead on your journey.

That's true of all the characters whose lives we've looked at here. As men and women, we tend to concentrate on where we have been or where we are going, but God focuses on who we are becoming in the process. It's easy to see the flaws in Abraham's life, but even the poor choices become like a polishing cloth in God's hands. If the whole point of the journey is to learn to become more like Jesus, which is to trust God 100 percent, then the places we have been or where we are headed seem to fade into insignificance.

I spent so much of my life trying to be a "good" Christian. That seems ridiculous to me now. I have never once seen a single sheep—and I grew up surrounded by them—trying to be a good sheep. The many sheep I've seen just go wherever their shepherd takes them. If they fall into a creek, they wait for the shepherd to get them out. If they're afraid of a stalking wolf, they know the shepherd has a mighty rod and staff to win any fight. They don't worry about where their next meal is coming from—they eat the grass at their feet, and when it's gone, the shepherd leads them to a new pasture.

That's how our Father wants us to live right now.

He has climbed the highest mountain to get to where he's prepared a place for us; one day the new pasture will be home.

Conclusion

We're Going Home, into the Arms of God

One day, he stood up and I stood beside him. He began to make his way out of the ruins into the daylight. I didn't want to leave and begged him to stay, but he kept walking. I followed. I knew I could never be separated from him. As we stood in the sunlight I found the vista before me terrifying.

I can't do this, I said.

I know, he answered.

I don't want to do this, I said.

I know, he answered.

What will I do? I asked.

Just follow me, he said.

Where are we going? I asked.

We're going home.

One of the advantages of flying as much as I do in each calendar year is that I accumulate a lot of frequent flyer miles. Usually Barry, Christian, and I use them for free flights on vacation, but in 2009 I used mine to fly home to Scotland to see my mom. She turned eighty that year, and I wanted to be able to celebrate with her in person.

Since Christian was at camp with his school for a week in May, that seemed the perfect time to go. I booked my flight from Dallas, through Miami, to London, then on to Glasgow, Scotland; and reserved a car in Glasgow, anticipating drives to some of Mom's favorite haunts.

So on a beautiful morning in May, Barry and I waved Christian off on his bus to camp, I kissed Barry good-bye as he settled in to being a bachelor for the week, and I headed to the airport.

The flight to Miami was uneventful, but as we landed I could see storm clouds rolling in and wondered if the London flight might be delayed. We were about two hours late in leaving, but the captain assured us that we would make up much of that time en route.

I slept for a few of the nine hours and felt pretty good when we touched down in London at seven o'clock the following morning. Soon I had transferred terminals and was on a British Airways flight heading north to Glasgow.

I love landing in Glasgow because if it's a clear morning, as it was that day, you get a wonderful view of green fields and very white sheep. As we touched down, I saw many of the spring lambs jumping and playing in the morning air, and I'm convinced they were *baa*ing with a Scottish accent.

I picked up my luggage, excited to be in my homeland, and headed to the car rental counter. I had specified on my booking that I needed a vehicle with an automatic transmission and wanted it by 11 a.m., and all had been confirmed. There was just one man ahead of me in line, so once he had been given his keys, I moved up to the counter and gave the assistant my confirmation sheet.

Now, if you have ever heard a very strong Glasgow accent, you might want to insert it into this next section. If not, perhaps you could rent the movie *Braveheart* as a reference tool.

Oh Dear!

"Good morning," I said to the woman behind the counter.

"Aye hello, hen," she replied. (No reference to poultry of any kind was intended here. *Hen* is simply a Scottish form of addressing a woman.) She looked at my sheet and then at me and said, "Oh dear!"

"Is there a problem?" I asked.

"You want an automatic?"

"Thank you, yes," I replied. "That's what I booked."

"Oh dear!" was all she managed.

"Is there a problem?"

"I've no got wan," she said. ("I do not have one.")

"But that's what I reserved," I said.

"Aye, I know," she agreed.

"But you don't have it?" I was beginning to feel frustrated.

"Naw, hen," she said. "Do you no want a stick shift?"

"I can't drive those," I told her.

"Why did ye no learn that?" she asked, apparently amazed at my ineptitude.

"I don't really know," I said.

She fumbled for something to say. "Oh dear," she managed again.

"I'm just wondering," I said, "what's the point of confirming something if when you get here, you don't have it?"

"Aye, I know, that's a good point," she agreed. We appeared to be at an impasse.

"Do you have any suggestions as to what I might do?" I asked.

"Aye, I do. See that wee shop over there?" she said. "Away and sit doon and have a wee cup of coffee."

Like a sheep that had been abandoned by her flock, I went and sat "doon" and had a very large cup of coffee. After about thirty minutes I wandered back to be greeted by this exuberant statement: "Great news, hen, I've got ye a car!"

It was an unusual experience to see an employee of a car rental company so overjoyed that she had actually located one. One got the feeling that this was something of a rare moment. But

I didn't say that. I joined in the celebration and took the keys with profound gratitude.

Home!

The drive from Glasgow to Ayr only takes about forty minutes. When you crest the last hill that takes you down into Ayrshire, you catch your first glimpse of the ocean. I love that view. Whether in summer or winter, that vista tells me I am home.

Of course, true home is where the heart is, as the adage goes, and so passing the ocean, I looked for my mother's house. My mom lives in a lovely stone cottage on the same street where she lived as a child. I find it hard to believe that she is eighty. But as I saw her standing at the door, waiting to welcome me inside, I saw my grandmother in her posture and in her sweet smile. It seemed as if the last twenty years in particular had suddenly galloped past.

I am in that interesting baby boomer place now, where I am watching my mother becoming more frail every month, even as I am seeing my son grow taller and stronger. One, in many ways, is finishing a journey as the other is just beginning.

I want to enjoy both.

With my mom, I had such a wonderful week. We looked at old photographs and talked and talked and talked. We drove into the countryside, ate lunch at local farms and garden centers, and talked some more.

On the Saturday of that week, my brother Stephen drove up from Cambridge, England, to spend the day with us, a real treat for me as I hadn't seen him in some five years. He's three years younger than I, very tall and very smart, with a wicked sense of humor. I adore my brother.

I was loving this sweet reunion with my family, especially Sunday morning, when Mom, Stephen, and I sat in my mom's regular pew in Ayr Baptist Church. As a family, we have been members of this church for generations, so I looked around for all the familiar faces. Although there were many I recognized, several significant faces were gone.

I felt the loss of three men in particular: Jim Martin, Peter Douglas, and Albert Clark—pillars of our church since I was a child, now all finished with their journey and home free. I thought about the way each of these men had lived their lives, how they had sacrificed and worked so tirelessly behind the scenes for so long serving God and his people. These men are heroes of mine, but so often no one noticed what they did. Well, that's not true— Someone missed absolutely nothing.

There Will Come a Day!

A day is coming that we don't talk about very often in the church; but for me, the awareness of it changes everything about our day-to-day lives. It is the day that will reveal what our journey looked like—and why trusting God now is so important.

God has always known us, inside and out; and on that day, we will know ourselves. Everything that is true about us will be revealed in the light of Christ. Paul writes about it in his second letter to the church in Corinth. It's such a key passage that I've shown it in two different translations:

> So we are always confident, knowing that while we are at home
> in the body we are absent from the Lord. For we walk by faith,
> not by sight. We are confident, yes, well pleased rather to be
> absent from the body and to be present with the Lord.

Therefore we make it our aim, whether present or absent, to be well pleasing to Him. For we must all appear before the judgment seat of Christ, that each one may receive the things done in the body, according to what he has done, whether good or bad. (2 Corinthians 5:6–10)

That's why we live with such good cheer. You won't see us drooping our heads or dragging our feet! Cramped conditions here don't get us down. They only remind us of the spacious living conditions ahead. It's what we trust in but don't yet see that keeps us going. Do you suppose a few ruts in the road or rocks in the path are going to stop us? When the time comes, we'll be plenty ready to exchange exile for homecoming. But neither exile nor homecoming is the main thing. Cheerfully pleasing God is the main thing, and that's what we aim to do, regardless of our conditions. Sooner or later we'll all have to face God, regardless of our conditions. We will appear before Christ and take what's coming to us as a result of our actions, either good or bad. (2 Corinthians 5:6–10 MSG)

The day that Paul is referring to in 2 Corinthians is not the judgment that will take place at the Great White Throne. That day is referred to in Revelation 20:11–12:

I saw a Great White Throne and the One Enthroned. Nothing could stand before or against the Presence, nothing in Heaven, nothing on earth. And then I saw all the dead, great and small, standing there—before the Throne! And books were opened. Then another book was opened: the Book of Life. The dead were judged by what was written in the books, by the way they had lived. (MSG)

On that day the Book of Life will be opened and anyone who has trusted in Christ and had their name written in the book will live forever and those who rejected Christ will be condemned and separated from Christ forever.

That day is the Day of Judgment. That is not the day Paul is talking about in 2 Corinthians. What Paul is writing about is the day when every Christian will stand before Christ and the contents of our hearts and souls will be seen. We will not have to answer for our sins on that day—those were covered at Calvary. We will have to give an account to Jesus of how we have lived our lives, why we made the choices we made, and what we held in our hearts that only he could see.

I Can Only Imagine!

Only recently did this truth hit me between the eyes. I have been attending church since I was a baby, and I am currently working to complete my master's degree in theology, but it never sank in before that one day I will stand by myself before the Lamb of God and my life will be unveiled.

That is staggering to me. If I did good things, but for terrible motives, Scripture makes it clear that those things will burn into nothing at my feet. When, by God's grace, I chose to love and serve and trust, no matter how dark the night was, those things will be revealed as gold and jewels:

> For no one can lay a foundation other than that which is laid, which is Jesus Christ. Now if anyone builds on the foundation with gold, silver, precious stones, wood, hay, straw—each one's work will become manifest, for the Day will disclose it, because it will be revealed by fire, and the fire will test what sort of work

each one has done. If the work that anyone has built on the foundation survives, he will receive a reward. If anyone's work is burned up, he will suffer loss, though he himself will be saved, but only as through fire. (1 Corinthians 3:11–15 ESV)

As sobering as this passage is, it also gives me strength and courage to live my life in light of that day. I used to misunderstand this passage, thinking the Day of Judgment would be one of those terrible days when Jesus would confront us with our secrets or hidden sins. After all, everyone's work will be revealed by fire.

But this passage has nothing to do with that. The Day of Judgment will be a great leveling of the church. Some of us, and I include myself in this crowd, have been given wonderful opportunities to serve Christ on very public platforms. Others, like the men I mentioned from my home church and many others, serve in quiet ways that receive little applause. On Judgment Day, Christ will reveal to us what is true about each one of us, and in the tribunal of the Lamb of God our lives will be examined, sifted, and weighed in the balance.

For some of us who have trusted Christ as Savior, but lived for ourselves, our life's work will burn up at our feet, and there will be nothing left. We will enter heaven but have nothing to place into the nail-pierced hands of Christ. For others, names perhaps that no one but Jesus knows, the fire will reveal gold and silver and precious stones. They will be placed into a crown and those who are given that crown will have the unspeakable joy of laying it at the feet of Jesus.

It doesn't matter what assignment we are given on this earth, what matters is our heart in the midst of the assignment.

Do you see how that changes everything?

So you didn't get the dream job or your marriage is disappointing or you feel as if no one really values what you do—none of that will matter. Rather, all you will care about is how you chose to live this day, and how you chose to live today will be revealed on *that* day.

When I stand before the Lamb of God and finally look into Jesus' eyes, I want my life to have become a thing of beauty—not because I got it all right but because with all my heart I trusted God.

The Swing

As I write, I am fifty-two years old. If I could sit beside that ten-year-old girl on the swing in the park, what would I tell her?

I would tell her she is beautiful.

I would tell her she is loved.

I would tell her not to be afraid when the road gets bumpy, because she is never alone.

I would tell her when she ends up in a psychiatric hospital it's just another stop on the path, a place to learn not to be afraid to lose what seems to matter because she will find what really matters.

I would tell her that she will fall down and she will get back up again, and she will fall and she will get back up again.

I would tell her that God can be fully trusted with her hopes and her dreams, her fears and her failures.

I would tell her then: swing as high as you can.

I saw Heaven and earth new-created. Gone the first Heaven, gone the first earth, gone the sea. I saw Holy Jerusalem, new-created, descending resplendent out of Heaven, as ready for God as a bride for her husband. I heard a voice thunder from the Throne: "Look! Look! God has moved into the neighbor-hood, making his home with men and women! They're his

people, he's their God. He'll wipe every tear from their eyes.
Death is gone for good—tears gone, crying gone, pain gone—
all the first order of things gone." The Enthroned continued,
"Look! I'm making everything new." (Revelation 21:1–5 MSG)

Notes

Introduction: Swinging in the Arms of God

1. Sheila Walsh, *Honestly* (Grand Rapids: Zondervan, 1997).

Chapter 3: The Hunger to Belong

1. Sheila Walsh, *Let Go* (Nashville: Thomas Nelson, 2009).
2. Gail Hyatt, 4 June 2009, www.twitter.com/gailhyatt

Chapter 4: A Broken Dream Becomes a Beautiful Life

1. As quoted in Glenn Van Ekeren, *Speaker's Sourcebook II* (New Jersey: Prentice Hall, 1994), 279.

Chapter 5: Why the Pain?

1. George R. Beasley-Murray, *Word Biblical Commentary* (Nashville: Thomas Nelson, 1999), 188.
2. General. Rabbinical Writings. 100, 64a.
3. Rudolph Schnackenburg, *The Gospel According to St. John* (Grand Rapids: Eerdmans, 1990).
4. Sheila Walsh, *Get Off Your Knees and Pray* (Nashville: Thomas Nelson, 2008).
5. R. H. Fuller, as quoted in George R. Beasley-Murray, *Word Biblical Commentary* (Nashville: Thomas Nelson, 1999), 194.
6. Sarah Young, *Jesus Calling: Enjoying Peace in His Presence* (Nashville: Integrity, 2004), April 16.

Chapter 6: Into the Darkness to Find the Light

1. "O Love That Will Not Let Me Go," words by George Matheson, written in 1882. Quoted at www.cyberhymnal.com

Chapter 7: The Life of Christ in Us

1. David Watson, *Fear No Evil* (London: Hodder and Stoughton, 1984), 8.
2. Ibid., 171.
3. Ibid.

Chapter 9: Trusting God with Your Dreams

1. R. T. Kendall, *God Meant It for Good* (Charlotte, N.C.: Morningstar, 1986), 71.
2. John Norton, *The Life and Death of John Cotton*, 1659.
3. R. T. Kendall, *God Meant It for Good*, 71.

Chapter 11: Trusting God When You Have a Lot to Lose

1. Wes Howard-Brook, *Becoming Children of God: John's Gospel and Radical Discipleship* (Eugene, OR: Wipf and Stock, 2003), 29.
2. *Nelson's New Illustrated Bible Dictionary* (Nashville: Thomas Nelson, 1995).

Chapter 12: Trusting God with Your Journey

1. Iain M. Duguid, *Living in the Gap Between Promise and Reality* (Phillipsburg, New Jersey: P&R Publishing, 1999), 59.

Discussion Guide

1. "Jesus didn't come to get you out of the pain of life," Walsh writes in chapter 1. "He has come to live *in you* through it." Name some of the places where you've been troubled or frightened in life, where your trust has been shaken that God has a plan and purpose for you.

2. How have you sensed or seen the presence of Jesus in those troubled places—or not? What do his care and providence mean to you? How would you define the care of Christ?

3. Imagine three ways things might be different for you in those hard places if you weren't waiting, as Walsh says she was, "for the other shoe to drop."

4. How would you react to a letter like the one Walsh received from someone unknown and carrying amazing, though mysterious, promises?

5. Proverbs 3:5 says to trust in the Lord and put away your own understanding. What did Walsh find this meant for her when doctors confirmed her first child would be seriously handicapped? What does this Scripture mean to you?

6. Do you wrestle with the fear of being known by others? How so, or why not?

7. What wounds, old or fresh, lie at the root of any fear that keeps you from wanting to be known? If that wound is too unspeakable right now, make a note of how that wound makes you feel. Ask someone you love to pray over that note, or keep that note in your Bible and pray over it.

8. In the struggle to trust, when there seems to be no encouragement, are you tempted to put your life on hold? How can you not? What happens if you do or don't?

9. What keeps you from becoming bitter and unable to trust when it seems that God is silent or that a dream or desire of your heart is breaking, languished, or disappearing?

10. In chapter 5, Walsh recounts how Jesus brought Lazarus back from the dead, and how that event made Jesus "unmanageable," dangerous, and threatening to the Pharisees. How is this like the way many others perceive the person who is enlivened to trust?

11. So let's say you've exercised trust in a situation, and you share with friends the remarkable news, but they don't want to hear it. How does this make you feel? What do you say or do?

12. "Sometimes I have to work hard to remind myself of things I know to be true," Walsh writes in chapter 6. What do you do in times like this in order to find reasons to trust?

13. Saul believed he had given his life to serving God and yet one day, on that road to Damascus, found himself rebuked by God. How could he have believed himself to be so right and yet have been so wrong?

14. Living a quiet life as Tabitha did of justice, mercy, and service to God can be lonely and forsaken. How can you know that your trust in these good measures is right, appreciated, and valued? Does knowing make your trust in these services any more valuable or not?

15. What does it look like in your life, as Walsh writes about in chapter 7, to reach out "when it makes you uncomfortable"?

16. In chapter 8, Walsh talks about walking along the shoreline while contemplating an unexpected, overwhelming turn in her career. What choices have you faced when on the edge of something? Do you wait for God to take away fear before you move into the unknown, or do you wade through your fear and see what God will do?

17. Where do you find the strength to take that leap of faith? Do you think courage is a gift or that the skills of trusting can be learned (and what kind of skills would be involved)?

18. Do you think moments of disaster in your life are part of God's plan for you?

19. What does Joseph's story in chapter 9 tell you about how trust requires forgiveness?

20. Is there a point where you can go beyond being able to ever trust again?

21. Not trusting God cost Samson his hair, his eyesight, and his freedom. What did it cost him when he finally trusted God? Is such trust worth the cost?

22. The influential men, like Joseph of Arimathea, who witnessed Jesus being accused before Pilate, could have spoken out about the wrong they witnessed. How do you summon courage and trust for justice when you see wrongdoing?

23. When is it an act of trust to keep your faith a secret?

24. How can you use failure, like Abraham, to increase your trust?

25. Who can you trust 100 percent? Why do you believe this?

26. What can you tell yourself in future moments of doubt and fear in order to summon trust?

Bible Study

W elcome! I am so pleased and honored that you have chosen
this book. Trust has been one of the key themes of my life,
especially when it comes to my relationship with the Father. I
believe that if we can learn to rest in his trust, so many of the
things that plague us from day to day will dwindle from torrential
storms to light drizzles. And I don't mean to say they will get easier
but that God's inexhaustible love and concern for us will so over-
shadow the day-to-day pressures. Or even the lifelong struggles
we battle.

The purpose of this Bible study is to take you deeper into the
message of *Beautiful Things Happen When a Woman Trusts God*. But
it is also designed to lead you deeper into your own specific need
for trust. And, of course, I hope to take you deeper into the Bible
and what it shows us about trust. My great hope and prayer is that
you will engage deeply with God's Word as you pay attention to
your own internal responses.

This study can be used by individuals or small groups. If
you're anything like me, sharing a journey of growth with close
friends is richer and, at times, easier because you have someone
to lean on. If at all possible, I encourage you to go through this
study with people you know, sharing your responses and learning to trust one another as you all learn to trust the Father more.

Finally, you'll notice there's a consistent rhythm to each
study chapter. "Find," "Feel," and "Follow" sections will lead you
through three purposeful stages. The first, "Find," is meant to
get you instantly into more Bible passages and will have a reading
assignment or two from God's Word. (Don't worry! They are brief
and hand-picked to intentionally deepen the message from the

book. No one's going to ask you to read Leviticus in a night.)

The second, "Feel," will lead you through responses to the book and to God's Word. This section is designed to help you find where you stand on the spectrum of trust.

The third, "Follow," will help you take your previous learning and turn it into new trust and obedience.

Oh, one last thing before you begin, I intentionally chose to omit writing lines from this study, so you'll need to have a journal handy. The reason for this being that I wanted you to have more depth in the study instead of writing space. I hope you find that to be the right choice as you move ahead.

Okay, so, without further ado, let's get started. May God be beside you as you begin this study and continue the lifelong process of trusting in him.

—Sheila Walsh

Why Are You So Afraid?

I wonder what comes to your mind when you hear the word *courage*? As a follower of Christ my heart is first drawn to him and stays there for a while. Matthew records in his gospel the following words of Jesus, "Walk with me and work with me—watch how I do it. Learn the unforced rhythms of grace" (11:29, MSG). Christ invites us to watch how he lived his life on earth and learn from him. Perhaps there is no more telling or teaching moment than his recorded dialogue with his Father in Gethsemane: "Going a little ahead, he fell on his face, praying, 'My Father, if there is any way, get me out of this. But please, not what I want. You, what do *you* want?'" (Matthew 26:39 MSG).

Here Christ makes it clear that courage must start with truth. As he cried out to his Father, Jesus showed us that he was afraid. We will never understand this side of eternity what it cost Christ to take on himself all the sin of a broken planet. But just as our devastation began in a garden with Adam and Eve, so our restoration began in Gethsemane. Having poured out his heart to his Father, Christ turned to face all that was ahead. That is courage.

Find

This is the way God works. Over and over again He pulls our souls back from certain destruction so we'll see the light—and *live* in the light!

—Job 33:29–30 MSG

- What does this verse say to you about courage?

Read Joshua 1:1–9.
- For what reason did Joshua need courage?
- How many times was he told to be courageous? Why do you think he was given this instruction repeatedly?

- Consider your present situation and rewrite Joshua 1:1–9 as if God were speaking to you. What instructions would he give and how many times would he repeat those instructions?
- Describe a time when you demonstrated great courage or a time when you needed more courage.
- "Jesus didn't come to get you out of the pain of life; he has come to live in you through it" (p. 2). How have you found this to be true in your life?

Feel

- You might have gone through some difficult times in your life. List some of the feelings you have had.
- Describe the role of your faith in facing your struggles. How would you describe your courage?
- What is one situation you are facing right now that causes your heart to race and your emotions to spin out of control?

Follow

- What do you believe God wants you to do in response to the situation you described in the previous question?
- How can God work through your friends, family members, and church to encourage and support you as you deal with this situation?
- What do you want God to do in your life through this study?
- What do you need to change in your life so you can be more focused on God and less focused on the situation you are facing?
- Summarize the instructions of Joshua 1:1–9 by completing the following statement:
  Because God said _____,
  I will _____.
- In your journal, write a prayer expressing your desires. Throughout the coming week, use this prayer as part of your conversation with God.

An Open Door

O ne of the things that's important to me as I study the Bible is to read verses in context of what was actually happening when they were written. It's tempting to simply pull out a verse like a rabbit from a magician's hat and apply it to our situation, but if we read in context I believe the message will run far deeper.

In Isaiah 43:18–19 we read, "Remember not the former things, nor consider the things of old. Behold, I am doing a new thing; now it springs forth, do you not perceive it?" (ESV).

These words were written to God's people held captive in Babylon. It was one of the lowest moments in their history. Isaiah prophesies about the coming captivity and exile and yet reminds the people that God is a God of love and he will bring them home. It is one more picture in the Old Testament foreshadowing the coming Christ who will deliver us from our sin and brokenness. In these two verses God is saying, *Don't look back to the time when I delivered your ancestors from Egypt, I am a God who delivers over and over again.*

You may find yourself in a place of brokenness at the moment, and even though God has delivered you before, you can't imagine how he will do it again as your situation is very different. Take your eyes off the past and fix them on Christ whose mercies are new every morning.

Find

Do not remember the former things, nor consider the things of old. Behold, I will do a new thing; now it shall spring forth; shall you not know it?

—Isaiah 43:18–19

· What does this verse say to you about God's ability to heal your brokenness?

Read Luke 4:18–21.

- Jesus quoted from the Book of Isaiah and made a declaration regarding the brokenhearted. Read this passage substituting your name for "the poor," "the brokenhearted," "the captives," "the blind," and "those who are oppressed." How does this passage speak to your life?
- Describe a time when you started over. How did that experience make you feel? What were the positive emotions you dealt with? What were the negative emotions you faced?
- "Good grief!" I said. "Lord, this is not funny. I have no idea what to do here!" (p. 13). Have you ever had an experience that caused you to say something like this? If so, describe that experience.

Feel

- What do you think is the difference between experiencing brokenness and your life being broken?
- How can you find hope in the midst of your brokenness? How do you feel about yourself when you are broken before God? How does he feel about you?
- Take a few moments and list some of the Scripture passages that have been most encouraging to you.

Follow

Read Sheila's letter on page 17.

- What does this letter say to you? What is God saying to you right now?
- Describe a time when you have heard the Lord say, "Just follow me."
- What encouragement can you give to someone who is struggling with the consequences of previous poor choices?
- How can you better follow God in the days ahead?
- Summarize the instructions of Luke 4:18–21 by completing the following statement:

  Because Jesus said _____,

  I will _____.

- In your study journal, write a prayer expressing your thankfulness to God for healing your brokenness. Throughout the coming week, use this prayer as part of your conversation with God.

THREE

THE HUNGER TO BELONG

If you abide in my word, you are truly my disciples,
and you will know the truth, and the truth will set you free.

—JOHN 8:31–32 (ESV)

Jesus spoke these words to a group of Jews who had been listening to
his teaching and identified themselves as those who believed in him.
Like many, they misunderstood what Jesus was talking about. When
they thought of freedom, they thought of what they could see—political
freedom, situational freedom. I understand that. For many years I
thought, "If I could just get away from this person or this situation, then
I would be free." The only trouble was that everywhere I went, I took
"me" with me. The freedom that Christ offers is far greater than a relo-
cation offer, it is an internal revolution. When, by God's grace, you face
all that is true about who you are and who you are not, and in that same
moment realize that you are totally loved by God, that is a freedom that
can be found nowhere else apart from Christ.

What I have learned is that freedom and transparency walk hand in
hand. To the level that we are willing to be known, to be seen, then at
that depth we can be set free from the things that have defined us apart
from Christ. It is risky to be known but it is what we were made for and
anything less is not freedom. You will know the truth and the truth will
set you free. It is a promise.

Find

The strength of the fatherless was crushed. Therefore snares are
all around you, and sudden fear troubles you.

—JOB 22:9–10

· Describe a situation when your words have been similar to the words
  in the verse above.

240

Read John 8:31–36.

- Why is it so important to be transparent with other people?
- God knows everything about us, so why is it important that we be transparent before him?
- Consider the questions below and respond to one or more of them:

  * What is it that I am afraid people might find out about me?
  * Why do I keep people at a distance?
  * Why do I assume that if I let people in they would be disappointed and leave?
  * Why do I fear rejection so intensely that I remove myself from the equation before anyone else gets to "vote me off the island"?

- Paul said, "Bear one another's burdens, and so fulfill the law of Christ" (Galatians 6:2). List some people who need you to bear their burdens and those people who have helped carry your burdens. Select one or more people on the list and, if possible, write personal notes of thanks or encouragement.

Feel

- "There are many different reasons we feel a sense of shame, but how we then behave seems very much the same. If we believe there is something deep inside of us that others would reject, we hold ourselves back or simply vote ourselves out of life. This can lead to depression, addictions, bitterness, and despair" (p. 31). Why do you think this isn't the life Christ wants for you?
- What comes to mind when you think about belonging? Be honest about your feelings.
- Describe a time when you have listened to a song or watched a scene in a movie and suddenly you are overwhelmed by feelings out of proportion to what is happening around you. How did that experience make you feel?
- What do you think God is trying to say to you through those experiences?

- Jesus issues an invitation to anyone who has finally come to the place where she is tired of pretending that everything is fine. Is this an offer you are willing to accept? Why or why not?

Follow

- God knows everything about you and loves you. What is keeping you from trusting him with your past and following him?
- Describe the spiritual breakthrough you would like to experience right now.
- Summarize the instructions of John 8:31–36 by completing the following statement:
  Because Jesus said _____,
  I will _____.
- Now write a prayer asking God to give you the breakthrough you described above. Keep praying the prayer and believing God for the answer as you spend time with him in the days to come.

FOUR

A Broken Dream
Becomes a Beautiful Life

There were many things in Anna's life that were disappointing. She lost her husband at a very early age, and she had no children. Much of what we know about Anna is by implication rather than direct knowledge. That she was allowed to occupy one of the temple apartments speaks volumes about her character. Her world was very much a male-dominated one where women were expected to be silent and unobtrusive. One of the key words that I see in Anna's life is *focus*. She didn't look back with regret but rather she looked forward with hope. That one thing alone could change the way we live. Think of the wasted energy we expend on regret. Obviously, grief plays a very necessary part in our lives, but grief adds to the tragedy when we allow it to define us. When grief defines us we forego the opportunity to truly live again. Although Anna knew heartache and loss, she focused on hope. When Paul wrote his first letter to the young Timothy he identified himself as, "Paul, an apostle of Christ Jesus by command of God our Savior and of Christ Jesus our hope" (1:1 ESV). That is how Anna lived her life, waiting patiently for Christ who is our hope.

It wasn't just her past that was harsh, for Anna lived under the cruel reign of Herod the Great. We know, too, that there was a lot of corruption in the priesthood. Just as today when we struggle with those who disappoint us in government or the pulpit, we have to choose where to focus our attention. Where are you focusing your attention as you wait on God's promise to you?

Find

Anna the prophetess was also there, a daughter of Phanuel from the tribe of Asher. She was by now a very old woman. She had been married seven years and a widow for eighty-four. She never left the Temple area, worshiping night and day with her fastings and prayers. At the very time Simeon was praying, she showed up, broke into an anthem of praise to God, and talked about the child to all who were waiting expectantly for the freeing of Jerusalem.

—LUKE 2:36–38 MSG

- How would you rate your patience? Place an X on the line below.
- Very patient ←————————————————→ Very impatient

Read Isaiah 40:25–31.
- What is the byproduct of waiting on the Lord?
- Take a closer look at verse 31. In what area of life do you need strength? What is God saying to you through this passage?
- What dream has God planted deep inside you? What prevents you from realizing that dream?
- Read the Scripture passage above. How would you have felt if you had been in Anna's situation?
- Fill in the blanks in the statement that follows:
  This stinks. I expected to be _____. I expected to have _____. All the rules seem to be changing. I _____! What do you expect God to do about your situation?
- "Anna dedicated her whole life to immersing herself in the Word of God and in his presence and sharing his Word with other women who came to the temple" (p. 46). Based on what Anna did, what should you do in response to your situation?

Feel
- Anna had every reason to feel hopeless and useless. Yet, she believed God's promise that she was valuable to him. How do you know you are valuable to God? How does that make you feel?
- Anna prayed that the Messiah would come. For what are you praying and what do you expect to happen when that prayer is answered?

- For what are you watching? How do you expect God to overwhelm your life?

Follow

- What is the role of your ongoing relationship with God in regards to your personal and spiritual expectations?
- How do you discern God's guidance from your feelings or the advice of others?
- Summarize the instructions of Isaiah 40:25–31 by completing the following statement:
  Because God said _____,
  I will _____.
- Now write a prayer expressing your desire to wait for God's answer to your prayers. Use this prayer as part of your daily time with God and as an expression of your desire to live with God-honoring patience as you wait for him to reveal his plan to you.

FIVE

WHY THE PAIN?

J esus never seems to show up when we expect him to. Think of what we know of the encounters recorded between Jesus and Mary, Martha, and Lazarus. One time he appeared to show up too early and the next, what to them seemed far too late. Luke records in his account that Jesus and the twelve disciples arrived in Bethany for a meal and Martha was not quite ready for them (10:38–42). This is the famous passage where Martha gets upset with Mary for sitting at Jesus' feet instead of continuing to help her. (It's interesting to me that the Greek translation of 10:39 includes the word *also*, but only the NKJV and NASV carry the word, making it clear that Mary had helped but now wanted to listen as Jesus taught.)

The next encounter, Jesus does not come when they call for him and that is far more devastating. What I learn from both vignettes is that Jesus' sole purpose was to do whatever brought honor to his Father. That can be hard for us to understand. One mother prays for a sick child and the child recovers, another mother prays and the child dies—why? We tend to internalize the circumstances and wonder what we have done wrong. Jesus showed us that when we cry out, and we must, we cry out to our Father that his will be done.

Find

When Jesus saw her sobbing and the Jews with her sobbing, a deep anger welled up within him. He said, "Where did you put him?"

—JOHN 11:33–34 MSG

- How do you deal with life's disappointments or troubling circumstances? Are you emotional or quiet? Do you take action or become reserved? Describe a recent situation that has been the most trying.

Read Matthew 14:22–33.

· Peter exercised great faith in getting out of the boat. What caused Peter to start sinking?

· What did Jesus do about Peter's situation?

· What is causing you to sink and what do you think Jesus will do about your situation?

· Take a few moments and locate some Scripture passages that are especially encouraging to you. List those passages and write out one you would like to memorize.

· How does crying out to God affect your relationship with him? How do you think God feels when we cry out to him?

Feel

· Describe a time when you have asked God to intervene in a situation. How did you know God was involved?

· Did the situation turn out like you prayed it would? How did that make you feel?

· When he realized he was sinking, Peter cried out to Jesus. When you are sinking emotionally, to whom or what do you cry out?

· Based on your options for dealing with the most trying situation you are facing, how can you best glorify God in your response?

Follow

· What is the difference between crying out to God and simply crying? Which do you most often do and why?

· Consider Jesus' raising of Lazarus from the dead. In John 11:39, Martha expresses some doubts about Jesus' ability to raise her brother. Martha had more confidence in her knowledge than her Savior. What does your attitude toward the impossible say about your faith in Jesus Christ?

· Jesus restored Lazarus's life. Do you believe he can restore the quality of your life? Why or why not?

· "How many times have you, like Martha, struggled, wavered in despair—or sunk into it—not seeing what you expect from God in the here and now?" (p. 63). What are three things you can do daily to prevent sinking into despair?

- Summarize the instructions of Matthew 14:22–33 by completing the following statement:

Because Jesus _____,

I will _____.

- Now write a prayer expressing your desire to wait for God's answer to your prayers. Use this prayer as part of your daily time with God and as an expression of your desire to live with God-honoring patience as you wait for him to reveal his plan to you.

SIX

INTO THE DARKNESS
TO FIND THE LIGHT

H ave you ever been in a situation where the tables seemed to turn
on you in a moment? That's how it must have seemed for Saul. As
he started on his journey from Tarsus to Damascus he was very much
alive in his own mind, and Jesus was dead. Before he reached his destination, though, Jesus proved that he was alive and Saul may as well have
been dead. Why such a dramatic intervention by Christ? The light that
surrounded Saul was so blinding that it knocked him off his horse, then
he was plunged into utter darkness. It's as if Christ is saying, *This is who
I am and this is where you are. I am a fierce blazing light and you are crawling in the darkness.*

I smile now when I think of the pictures of Jesus that were shown to
me in Sunday school as a child. They portrayed a very mild-mannered,
almost pretty man. Christ's love is fierce. When he finds one whom he
loves living in blind conviction, he will do what it takes to bring that
person into the light. Once you have been brought from darkness into
light you are never the same. The more you see, the more you trust and
the more you love.

Find

When he got to the outskirts of Damascus, he was suddenly dazed by a
blinding flash of light. As he fell to the ground, he heard a voice: "Saul,
Saul, why are you out to get me?" He said, "Who are you, Master?"

—ACTS 9:3–5 MSG

- Before his conversion and name change, Saul (Paul) was passionate.
  After his conversion he was passionate. We can conclude that Paul was
  a passionate guy. God took Paul's passion and refocused it toward God's

purposes. What characteristics do you have that God can refocus for his purposes?

Read 1 John 3:1–3.
- Describe the depth of God's love for his children.
- What is the outcome of the hope we have (verse 3)?
- How can you purify yourself? What changes do you need to make in your daily routine so that you will be purified in your thoughts and actions?
- Reconsider Paul's life following his conversion. How did his past hinder his ministry? How did his past prepare him for ministry?
- Now think about your life. How does your past hinder your present life? How has your past equipped you to care for and encourage others around you?

Feel

- How do you feel when you consider yourself from God's perspective?
- What is there about you that God loves?
- Review *What Have I Done?* (pages 78–80 note: there are two sections with the same heading. This is a reference to the first one). God was using Stephen in incredible ways, but the religious people didn't like it. Why would religious people react negatively to God's work through someone like Stephen?
- Had you been in that situation, would you have sided with the religious people or with Stephen? Why?
- Stephen's stance for God ultimately cost him his life. What are you willing to sacrifice so that your life can be more honoring to God?
- When given the opportunity to defend himself publicly, Stephen spoke about Jesus Christ and his faith in God's Son. What do you talk about when you have a public platform?

Follow

- The more the early believers were persecuted, the more they were strengthened in their faith. Difficult times either drive us in the arms of Christ or force us into self-dependency. One is a source of strength; the other despair. How is your faith affected by the struggles you face?

· "Jesus is saying: Let go of whatever it is you are trying to hold onto. If you are trying to hold onto a life, a ministry, a position, or a career that doesn't please God, then let it die. Trust him, instead of yourself, to accomplish his will. If he is involved, then in his time, he will let what you let go bloom once again" (p. 88). What is your response to this statement?

· Paul was given a new name, a new purpose, and a reassigned passion. You, too, have been given a new name—God's child—a new purpose, and a reassigned passion. What do you think God is doing in your life right now?

· What does God want to do through your life?

· Summarize the instructions of 1 John 3:1–3 by completing the following statement:

Because the Bible says _____,

I will _____.

· Now write a prayer asking God to allow you to see yourself the way he sees you. Use this prayer as part of your daily time with God and as an expression of your desire to be used for his purposes.

SEVEN

THE LIFE OF CHRIST IN US

The fact that Tabitha is the only woman in the New Testament to be
given the title "disciple" is arresting to me. When you think of the
word *disciple*, what comes to mind? When I think of the twelve men that
Christ chose to share his three years of earthly ministry, it's clear that
they saw so much. They witnessed miracle after miracle. They sat with
Jesus as he shared things with them that the crowds did not get to hear.
They were there when Lazarus stumbled back into his own skin and into
daylight. They shared that last precious meal that Christ would eat on
earth and watched as he was dragged away to a mockery of a trial. They
lamented and hoped during his ultimate execution. They saw the resurrected Christ, heard his voice again. They looked into those eyes of
blazing love again.

Peter, who had once denied even knowing Christ, at his own crucifixion declared he was unworthy to die in the same manner as his Savior.
He asked, instead, to be crucified upside down. But what of Tabitha? She
didn't see any of that but she was called "disciple." She was called disciple because she "got it." She understood that whether you are in a
crowd that witnessed the spectacular or in a quiet room making clothes
for the destitute, every single thing you do matters when it is motivated
by a heart of love for Christ.

Find

Now there was in Joppa a disciple named Tabitha. . . . She was full of
good works and acts of charity. In those days she became ill and died,
and when they had washed her, they laid her in an upper room.... All
the widows stood ... weeping and showing tunics and other garments
that [Tabitha] made while she was with them. But Peter put them all
outside, and knelt down and prayed; and turning to the body he said,
"Tabitha, arise." And she opened her eyes, and when she saw Peter she

sat up. And he gave her his hand and raised her up. Then calling the saints and widows, he presented her alive.

—ACTS 9:36–37, 39–41 ESV

- Tabitha was a follower of Christ and her death saddened those who knew her. She was known for her faithfulness. If your life ended right now, for what would you be remembered?

Read Psalm 16.
- How would you characterize the mood of the psalmist as he wrote these words?
- On a scale of 1–10, with 10 being maximum, rate the psalmist's trust in God. __
- Using the same scale, rate your trust in God. __
- Explain any differences between the two ratings.
- Review verses 9–11 and rewrite them as your expression of your trust in God. Be completely honest as you express your trust.

Feel
- Think about your most recent experience with the death of a loved one or friend. What emotions did you experience as you lived through this experience?
- How did that experience affect your trust in God? Explain your response.
- Tabitha was well loved and those who loved her were not ready to say good-bye. Yet, she died. Why do you think the people sent for Peter?
- Peter had faith in God's ability to raise Tabitha because he had seen Jesus raise Jairus's daughter. What have you seen Jesus do that gives you assurance of his ability to intervene in your life in the future?

Follow
- The raising of Tabitha from the dead caused many people to put their faith in Jesus. What is Jesus doing in and through your life that would draw other people to have faith in him?

- "When we have had an encounter with the risen Christ, and he transforms our lives, he changes our hearts too. We *want* to serve, love, and show mercy—these things are evidence of a maturing faith, especially when the things that move the Son of God move our hearts too" (p. 109). To what extent does your lifestyle reflect Christ's transformational power? Do you want to serve, love, and show mercy? Why or why not?
- Summarize the instructions of Psalm 16 by completing the following statement:
  Because the psalmist said _____,
  I will _____.
- Now write a prayer expressing your desire to trust God even when the circumstances seem impossible. Use this prayer as part of your daily time with God and as an expression of your desire to follow him even when the path is uncertain.

EIGHT

TRUSTING GOD WITH YOUR FEAR

One of the most transforming truths I have embraced on my journey thus far is that whatever God calls me to do, he has already equipped me to do it. That sounds so obvious, so simple, and yet I believe we struggle to live that way. We live in a culture that quantifies giftedness, beauty, leadership by its own set of rules. In the Kingdom of God our culture's rules don't apply. Our culture looks at what appears to be true but God sees what is true. When God looks at a man or woman he sees who we are becoming in him. So God looked at Gideon cowering in the wine press and called him a mighty warrior. Jesus looked at Peter and said, "And I tell you, you are Peter, and on this rock I will build my church, and the gates of hell shall not prevail against it" (Matthew 16:18 ESV). This was before Peter denied even knowing Christ. This was before Peter disappeared into the night and left Christ to die. When Jesus looks into the heart of a man or woman he sees all of who we are and all of who we will become in him by trusting and taking the next step. So if God says move, I move. I trust who he knows me to be more than who I see myself as.

Find

One day the angel of GOD came and sat down under the oak in Ophrah that belonged to Joash the Abiezrite, whose son Gideon was threshing wheat in the winepress, out of sight of the Midianites. The angel of GOD appeared to him and said, "GOD is with you, O mighty warrior!" Gideon replied, "With *me*, my master? If GOD is with us, why has all this happened to us?"

—JUDGES 6:11–13 MSG

Read Judges 6:7–10.

· God reminded the Israelites of his goodness to them. If that passage had been written to you, what are some of the things God has done that he would have called for you to remember?

- The Israelites had seen God do some incredible things, yet they still rebelled against him and failed to trust him. Describe a time when you have been rebellious against God or refused to trust him. Why did you respond the way you did?

Read Proverbs 3:5–7.
- Rewrite these verses in your own words and then commit these verses to memory.

Feel

- You are going about your daily routine and you are greeted by an angel saying, "God is with you, O mighty warrior." How would that make you feel?
- We don't have experiences like that very often, so how do you know God is with you?
- Gideon said, "If God is with us, why has all of this happened to us?" How did Gideon's view of the situation compare to God's perspective?
- How does God's perspective of your life compare to your perspective of the things you are experiencing?

Follow

- In Judges 6:14, God asks Gideon, "Haven't I just sent you?" God's sending always includes his power because God never asks us to do something he doesn't equip us to do. In what area of life do you need to accept God's commission and depend upon his power?
- What keeps you from trusting God to empower you to do those things he asks you to do?
- Gideon recognized that God is peace. Is this a truth that is evident in your life? Explain your response.
- God uses external circumstances to get our attention. What is God using right now to get your attention?
- "The key to this transformation is found in Judges 6:34: 'God's Spirit came over Gideon'" (p. 127). What will happen in your life when God's Spirit comes over you?

- Gideon experienced victory because he did what God told him to do. If you want victory in your life, what are some things you must do?
- Summarize the instructions of Proverbs 3:5–7 by completing the following statement:

  Because the Bible says _____,

  I will _____.
- Now write a prayer expressing your desire to trust God more every day. Use this prayer as part of your daily time with God and as an expression of your desire to give God the honor and trust he deserves.

NINE

Trusting God with Your Dreams

The biggest question I have had to face in the last few years is this: Do I believe that God is in control? God is either sovereign all the time or he is not sovereign at all. If he is, and I believe he is, that means that nothing that happens to me is random but has passed through his hands of mercy and grace. That doesn't mean I believe God orchestrates evil to see how we will respond. God is love, and there is no evil in him at all. We live, however, in a fallen world where evil exists. But God has promised that no matter what we face, he will work for our good in the midst of it.

Joseph saw that. It was clear that his brothers hated him in the beginning and feared him at the end. Hatred and fear are both powerful weapons in the hands of an enemy but our God is bigger than our enemy. I believe that the greatest gift we can give our Father is to keep our focus on him even when the road becomes very dark. If you are a child of God, you are not a helpless victim. Like Joseph, you can face betrayal. But in God's perfect time your dream will be brought into the light.

Find

Joseph had a dream. When he told it to his brothers, they hated him even more.

—Genesis 37:5 MSG

- "God is more interested in what he is doing in you than through you" (p. 137). Why is this true?
- What God-sized dream is alive deep within you?

Read Genesis 37:2–8.
- How would you have felt toward Joseph if you had been one of his brothers?
- After Joseph interpreted his dream, why did his brothers respond so harshly?

- It is easy to doubt a dream and even begin to think the dream means nothing. How do you know the dream inside you was planted by God?

Feel

- Joseph was eventually thrown into a pit by his brothers. Have you ever been thrown into a pit? If so, by what?
- How did you feel while in that pit?
- To whom did you turn to be rescued from the pit?
- Joseph made his way to Egypt and experienced a series of highs and lows that led to his being put in charge of all of the grain in the land. His brothers, suffering the effects of the famine, approached him asking for food. If you had been Joseph in that situation, how would you have responded to your brothers? Why?
- Consider the following questions and respond to them honestly.

  * I say I trust God, but do I?
  * I say God is in control, but will I let go?
  * I say God is my deliverer, but will I allow him to vindicate me?
  * I say God is my defender, but do I still want to speak up for myself?

- Joseph had every right to seek revenge, but he offered his brothers forgiveness. What do Joseph's actions reveal about God's attitude toward us?

Follow

- "Think about your own life right now. Perhaps you started out with a dream of what you believed God would do with your life. Then life itself got in the way. Maybe even at this moment, you sit wounded, broken, wondering where God is.
- "God is here. He is right here with you. He never left you but at every turn in the road longs to show you what is inside your heart and set you free. You are not a victim of the whims of others, no matter how true that may feel. You are a beloved daughter of the King who is making

you into a person of greater and greater beauty as you learn to leave your dreams in his care" (p. 154). How can you reclaim your dream and get back on the path to being the woman God created you to be?

- Now write a prayer expressing your desire to let the dream God planted in you be reborn in your life. Use this prayer as part of your daily time with God and as an expression of your desire to pursue God's best for your life.

Is It Ever Too Late
to Start Again?

I would imagine for most women reading this book this chapter may appear to have the least connection to their lives. Think about it, if you have seriously messed up your life with one poor choice after another, it's not very likely that you would pick up a book with the title *Beautiful Things Happen When a Woman Trusts God*. But for those who might have, let me say this. If you sit right now with the reality of a stream of bad choices and you did pick up this book, then I think you are beginning to grasp the truth that with God it is never too late to start back on a good path. If there is one breath left in your body and you cry out to God, he will hear and receive you. Just ask the criminal executed beside Christ (Luke 23:43).

What about those you may have given up on? It could be a child who has walked away from everything you taught him and shows no sign of ever wanting to turn his heart back towards God. It's easy to despair in those moments, but trust asks us to keep bringing that person to the throne of grace. Whether it's one bad choice or a lifetime of bad choices, the Shepherd waits to lead us all home.

Find

And Samson cried out to GOD: "Master, GOD! Oh, please, look on me again. Oh, please, give strength yet once more, God!"

—JUDGES 16:28 MSG

Read 2 Corinthians 5:14–17.
· How does God's evaluation of us compare to the way the world judges people?

Read Judges 13:1–24.
· What does this story teach about God's ability and willingness to offer second chances?

- In what ways do you see doubt expressed by Manoah?
- Describe your need for a fresh start. In what area of life do you need a God-sized do-over?
- If you had a fresh start today, how would you live differently?

Feel

- Samson was born with a promise that would protect him throughout his life if he only lived up to the terms of the agreement. What are the terms of the agreement God makes with those who seek him?
- How does it make you feel to disappoint someone?
- How do you feel when you disappoint God?
- How do you think God feels when you disappoint him? Why?
- Samson made the mistake of trusting himself instead of trusting God. His mistake cost him. Have you ever made this mistake? If so, what did it cost you?

Follow

- Samson never intended for things to end up the way they did. It was the result of a series of bad choices. What guidance does God provide that will help us make wise choices?
- How passionate are you about making wise choices?
- How did God reveal himself and show his power through Samson?
- Samson's continual source of problems was his affection for women. What is the constant source of sin or temptation in your life?
- God offers us the opportunity to start over. Spend a few moments talking to God about your need for a fresh start and asking him to overwhelm your life with his presence. Write out your commitment to God.
- Summarize the instructions of 2 Corinthians 5:17 by completing the following statement:
  Because the Bible says _____,
  I will _____.
- Now write a prayer asking God to continue to renew you every day. Use this prayer as part of your daily time with God and as reminder that you are a new creation with a new purpose and destiny.

TRUSTING GOD WHEN YOU HAVE A LOT TO LOSE

I want you to imagine a scenario where you are interviewing a large group of women who have no involvement in the church. Your question to them is this, "When you hear the word *Christian*, what images come to your mind?" What kind of responses do you think you might receive? The answers might vary some by location. But if you took a slice out of all the responses you received, I'm sure you would hear a few of the same words:

- Judgmental
- Hypocritical
- Legalistic
- Out-of-touch

A long list of what we are "against."

It is a sad indictment when we are defined by what we stand against. What if we were instead known for the same passionate love that compelled God to send Christ to a broken world, a world beyond repair apart from him? I think at times we have lost the heart of the gospel, which is the love of God, and held on to what we perceive to be correct behavior.

I used a hairdresser for almost a year before he acknowledged that he had known from day one who I was. "I know that you were on Christian television, and I assumed I wouldn't like you. But you're not what I expected." I asked him what he expected. "Someone who judged me," he answered quickly. "But you accept me, you make me laugh." I took that as a compliment.

When Christ stepped into Nicodemus's world, he was not what Nicodemus expected. It shook every preconceived idea that he had.

Wouldn't it be a glorious challenge to step into our world today and *not be* what a watching world expects?

Find

There was a man of the Pharisee sect, Nicodemus, a prominent leader among the Jews. Late one night he visited Jesus and said, "Rabbi, we all know you're a teacher straight from God. No one could do all the God-pointing, God-revealing acts you do if God weren't in on it."

—JOHN 3:1–2 MSG

· What are some things you see happen that you know are the result of God's work in the world?

Read John 3:1–17.
· In his conversation with Nicodemus, Jesus spoke the most famous verse in the Bible (v. 16). Why did Nicodemus need to hear those words?
· Why do we need to hear those words?
· The people in Nicodemus's time had strong ideas about what the Messiah would look like and do. What are people looking for today?
· What is your responsibility when it comes to delivering the Messiah to the world?

Feel

· Jesus told Nicodemus that a person must be born again to see the kingdom of God. How did you feel when you were first born again?
· How has that feeling changed through the years?
· The first followers of Jesus had to give up everything to follow him. Today, many people view their faith as an add-on to an already busy life. What is the difference between giving up everything and viewing faith as another activity? Which description better fits you?
· The people in the first century had specific expectations of the Messiah. What do you expect the Messiah to do in your life?
· Have you ever been in a place where you knew you needed to speak up for Jesus? How did you feel and how did you respond?

- The early followers of Jesus were criticized and threatened because of their faith. How would persecution affect your faith? Would it be stronger or weaker as a result?

Follow

- "Nicodemus and Joseph had to leave behind everything they knew to start again in a new city, but they were starting with the experience of having seen Jesus with their own eyes and knowing him as the risen Son of God. What if you were called to follow God, too, leaving behind everything you have—but the call was your first introduction to the truth that God is real and personal? Would you start to trust him when you have no history with him?" (pp. 194–95). Why or why not?
- If you were certain your life would reach its full potential if you gave total control to Christ, would you be willing to give him control? Why or why not?
- Summarize the instructions of John 3:16 by completing the following statement:
  Because Jesus said _____,
  I will _____.
- Now write a prayer asking God to continue to remind you of your commitment to him and his promise of eternal life. Use this prayer as part of your daily time with God and as reminder that the most meaningful life you can live is the one lived for God and his purposes.

TWELVE

TRUSTING GOD WITH YOUR JOURNEY

Abraham's journey has taught me so much about what evolving trust looks like. It helps me see how patient and loving God is with us as we learn. It's unlikely that many of us in the next year will be asked to pick up everything we own and transfer across the country or across the world, but there are other kinds of pilgrimages. If we could shift our perspective to view each day as a spiritual pilgrimage, how would that change our lives?

What would it look like for you to get up every morning with the heart of a traveler? I understand that you have commitments and responsibilities, but those do not have to be the loudest voice in your day. Each morning when I get up, I pray, "Lord, I don't know where you are going today but, wherever it is, I'm coming with you."

On any regular day I know that I'll get up, make coffee and have some quiet time with Christ before I wake my son and take him to school. Then I'll come home, go to the gym, come home, take a shower, and do whatever is on the agenda for the day. But I do it with the heart of a pilgrim who asks, "Let me see with your eyes, let me hear with your ears, don't let me miss a moment with you on this journey home." In blue jeans or a ball gown, I am a pilgrim going home.

Find

GOD told Abram: "Leave your country, your family, and your father's home for a land that I will show you."

—GENESIS 12:1 MSG

· How would you respond if that instruction were given to you?
· What would make someone like Abraham follow those instructions?

Read John 1:35–51.

- When Jesus called the first disciples, they followed without delay. Why are we so reluctant to follow Christ the way the first disciples did?
- Jesus said, "Follow me." What did he mean by this command?
- How does his call to believers today compare to that call?

Feel

- We know that God created us and, according to Jeremiah 29:11, has a plan for our lives. How do you feel about turning over management of your life to God?
- The early disciples left behind their homes, professions, and possibly their families to follow Jesus. In other words, their faith was their first priority. If someone followed you for a week, what would she conclude is your first priority?
- How do you feel about that being your priority in life?
- What is something you think God might be asking you to do?
- In consideration of that matter, respond to the following questions:

  - Is God telling me to do this, or am I just imagining that because of my own wants?
  - What if I get this wrong?
  - If I miss God, will I have blown his plan for my life?
  - If it is God speaking here and I don't follow what I hear, will I miss his best for me?

- God had been preparing Abraham for his journey. What is God doing in your life to prepare you for his plans for you?
- Every place Abraham went he built an altar as a reminder of God's promises. What reminds you of God's promises to you?

Follow

- It's hard to follow an unknown path. But it is possible if we trust the guide. God wants to guide us on a path to an unbelievable future. A future that is built upon his promises to us and his power over our circumstances.

· Is that the kind of life you want?
· What is keeping you from accepting God's offer?
· Summarize the instructions of John 1:43 by completing the following statement:

Because Jesus said _____,

I will _____.

· Now write a prayer restating your commitment to follow Christ. Use this prayer as part of your daily time with God and as a reminder that because God created you, he has the best possible plan for you.

About the Author

Sheila Walsh has spoken to more than 4 million women at Women of Faith conferences around the country. She is the author of the award-winning Gigi, God's Little Princess series, the book and Bible study *Beautiful Things Happen When A Woman Trusts God*, and the upcoming new fiction trilogy Angel Song. Sheila lives in Frisco, Texas with her husband Barry and son Christian.

You can learn what Sheila is up to these days
by following her on Twitter and Facebook.

@SheilaWalsh
www.twitter.com/sheilawalsh
www.facebook.com/sheilawalshconnects